3-MINUTE PRAYERS

PRAYERS

for Women

Published by Barbour Books, an imprint of Barbour Publishing, Inc., 1810 Barbour Drive, Uhrichsville, Ohio 44683, www.barbourbooks.com

Our mission is to inspire the world with the life-changing message of the Bible.

Member of the
Evangelical Christian
Publishers Association

Printed in China.

3-MINUTE PRAYERS

for Women

Linda Hang

BARBOUR BOOKS

An Imprint of Barbour Publishing, Inc.

Introduction

Quiet down before God, be prayerful before him.
PSALM 37:7 MSG

These encouraging prayers are especially for those days when you are weary from the busyness of everyday life and your soul is longing for a quiet time of refreshment in the heavenly Creator's calming presence. Three minutes from your hectic day is all you'll need to fill your cup to overflowing with strength for life's journey.

- Minute 1: Read and reflect on God's Word.

- Minute 2: Pray, using the provided prayer to jump-start a conversation with God.

- Minute 3: Reflect on a question for further thought.

Although this book isn't meant as a tool for deep Bible study, each soul-stirring prayer can be a touchstone to keep you grounded and focused on the One who hears all your prayers. May this book remind you that the heavenly Father cares about everything you have to say. Go on...talk to Him today. He's ready and waiting to hear from you!

Prayer First

And rising very early in the morning, while it was still dark,
he departed and went out to a desolate place, and there he prayed.

MARK 1:35

Some days, before I'm even out of bed, my mind swirls with plans, to-do lists, worries. . .but I forget to come to You, my heavenly Father. I attempt to live life on my own, forgetting that You have promised to walk this earth beside me—sharing my burdens and offering Your wisdom and strength when mine will surely fail. Even if it is only five minutes on the knees of my heart before rolling out of bed, let my priority be time spent with You. May I follow Jesus' example to put prayer before any other pursuit for the day. Amen.

THINK ABOUT IT:

Do you make time for prayer in the same way you make
time for other activities—exercising, fixing hair or makeup,
perusing social media—in your morning routine?

Rest for Souls

"Come to me, all who labor and are heavy laden, and I will give you rest. Take my yoke upon you, and learn from me, for I am gentle and lowly in heart, and you will find rest for your souls."

MATTHEW 11:28-29

My deliverance. My rescue. My salvation. Thank You, Lord, for providing a way back to You. We have all fallen short of righteousness, but through the gift of Your Son's life, we can find rest for our souls. No more striving to live a perfect life—and failing. No more hoping that we're good enough—and realizing we aren't. Through Your incomprehensible love, we become children of the Most High. Christ's righteousness is ours; His yoke is light. As my heart overflows with gratitude, help me share Your love with others. Amen.

THINK ABOUT IT:

How will you find rest in God's gift of grace today?

Here for Now

So [Isaac] built an altar there and called upon the
name of the Lord and pitched his tent there.

GENESIS 26:25

Father, if there is one word to describe this life, it might be *impermanent.*
People come and go. We move from here to there. Even our emotions
shift from day to day. But You, Lord, will never change. Isaac built an
altar—an enduring reminder of You—and pitched his tent—a mark of a
transitory life. As I go through my life, help me build my faith. Help my
worship of You become the one steady point in an often-shifting world.
The apostle Paul's words echo in my mind: "The present form of this
world is passing away" (1 Corinthians 7:31). May I not cling to earthly
things but be ready to follow Your command. Amen.

THINK ABOUT IT:

Do your security and purpose come from eyes fixed
on God or in creating an earthly nest?

Stop and Know

*"Be still, and know that I am God. I will be exalted
among the nations, I will be exalted in the earth!"*

PSALM 46:10

Be still. A call to quiet my restless mind—to pause in my endless pursuits. *Know that You are God.* You are almighty. You are Lord. Regardless of what goes on in the world today, Father, I can be still and relish the knowledge that the God who created and controls the universe also resides in my heart. And Your plans will not be shaken—even when my fears shake me to the very core. Deepen my trust, Father; take my head knowledge to my heart so I can feel Your presence in my life, to be still and know that You are God. Amen.

THINK ABOUT IT:

Does stopping to reflect on God's omnipotence bring a sense of peace despite rocky circumstances in the world or your life?

"Someday My Prince Will Come"

For to us a child is born, to us a son is given; and the government
shall be upon his shoulder, and his name shall be called Wonderful
Counselor, Mighty God, Everlasting Father, Prince of Peace.

ISAIAH 9:6

Lord Jesus, how many stories center on a young prince rescuing a fair maiden? The good news is, we don't have to wait for Prince Charming to sweep us away from evil. An even greater Prince has already come! As our rescuer, our redeemer, You arrived on earth as a baby to save us from death. You are wise beyond anything humans can comprehend. You are powerful to accomplish Your will. You pour out Your love to us as our heavenly Father. You bring peace. Someday is now as we choose to follow You. Amen.

THINK ABOUT IT:

What do each of Christ's titles mean to you in your life?

The Good Portion

But the Lord answered her, "Martha, Martha, you are anxious and troubled about many things, but one thing is necessary. Mary has chosen the good portion, which will not be taken away from her."

LUKE 10:41–42

Father, how many times You must call to me as You did with Martha! When my anxious thoughts run circles in my head. . . When I am worried about all the day holds. . . May I hear You calling my name, not as a rebuke, but tenderly. You long for me to choose the one necessary thing—relationship with You. May I daily sit at Your feet and soak up Your words. May my focus be on You first, while all else takes second place. Remind me, Father, that what I invest in You will not be taken from me. Amen.

THINK ABOUT IT:

Do you identify more with Martha or
Mary—fretting or faith focused?

I Want Your Gift!

If the whole body were an eye, where would be the sense of hearing?
If the whole body were an ear, where would be the sense of smell?
But as it is, God arranged the members in the body,
each one of them, as he chose.

1 CORINTHIANS 12:17–18

Father, Christians are the hands and feet, the eyes and ears—the members of the body of Christ, each designed perfectly to spread Your glory. In Your wisdom, You have gifted me in specific and intentional ways. Sometimes I struggle with contentment, wishing I had a different gift. Forgive my jealousy, Father. Help me recognize my place. Help me rejoice in the *me* You created. Only I can fill the role You have appointed to me. And I can only blossom in my role through You. Amen.

THINK ABOUT IT:

In what ways can you appreciate and use the spiritual gifts
that God has graciously and purposely given you?

Escape Route

No temptation has overtaken you that is not common to man.
God is faithful, and he will not let you be tempted beyond your
ability, but with the temptation he will also provide the
way of escape, that you may be able to endure it.

1 CORINTHIANS 10:13

Father, sometimes I seem to struggle with the same temptations. But there is hope! I read in Your Word that You will provide a way out. Open my eyes to see the escape route. Reach out to me as I grasp for Your hand. Lift my focus from the temptation to You. I want to live a life of victory over sin. I know this is only possible through Your power. Alone, I will fail; together with You, I will overcome. Thank You for Your faithfulness. Amen.

THINK ABOUT IT:

How do the words of 1 Corinthians 10:13 encourage
you when you face temptation?

Laser Focused

He said, "Come." So Peter got out of the boat and walked on the water and came to Jesus. But when he saw the wind, he was afraid.

MATTHEW 14:29-30

Lord, I see myself in Peter. On good days I am confident, stepping into life with my eyes trained on You. But then the storm rolls in. The wind begins to blow. And my focus falters. I look away from You, and suddenly I am afraid. What joy there is in the rest of Matthew's account! Peter cries out—and You take hold of him. Be my rescue in the storms. But more than that, increase my faith so I will not doubt Your presence or Your power to calm the wind. May my eyes be ever focused on You, Father. Amen.

THINK ABOUT IT:

Like a pirouetting dancer always orienting her head to a single focal point, how important is it for Christians to remain focused on God?

Profitless

"And which of you by being anxious can add a single hour to his span of life?"

MATTHEW 6:27

Father, so many times I am reminded of this verse in my life. I worry—a lot—about something, and the "problem" I anticipate resolves itself easily or never surfaces at all. Or something else, something I never would have known to anticipate, ends up being a problem! My response is not to be a bundle of nerves perpetually, fearing life and what might catch me unawares. I need a daily reminder of the futility of worry, Father. You call me to a life of peace. Even if my world crumbles, my soul is safe with You. And You promise to walk with me through debris and clear paths alike. Thank You for Your presence. Amen.

THINK ABOUT IT:

Has worry ever had a positive or constructive influence on a difficult situation in your life?

Heaven Is Worth a Fortune

*"The kingdom of heaven is like treasure hidden in a field,
which a man found and covered up. Then in his joy he
goes and sells all that he has and buys that field."*

MATTHEW 13:44

It's so easy to lose sight of heaven, Lord. I'm bombarded by all that this world offers, and I begin to build my "kingdom" on earth. I forget that my life does not end here, but it continues forever with You. Am I willing to let go of all I have—materially and emotionally—to gain spiritual rewards that are beyond comprehension? Is the promise of heaven worth my all? Yes! Fix my heart on You, Father. Fill it with the joy of the man who sold everything in commitment to the treasure that awaits. Amen.

THINK ABOUT IT:

How can you develop a heart attitude of being
"all in" for Christ and His kingdom?

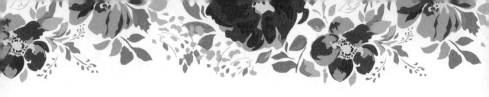

Prayers from Heaven

*"Simon, Simon, behold, Satan demanded to have you,
that he might sift you like wheat, but I have prayed
for you that your faith may not fail."*

LUKE 22:31-32

Lord, this world is full of trials. Refining trials. Trials that test me but ultimately make me purer. Though Peter failed by denying You, his faith survived. I wonder if, looking back, he was encouraged or comforted by Your prayer—to know that the God who sees all—who knew Peter's weaknesses beforehand—prayed for his faith victory. As I go through my own life's trials, pray for me, Lord. I need all the support I can get! Too often I'm like Peter, failing again and again and again. But my faith endures. Praise God, I have an advocate in You! Amen.

THINK ABOUT IT:

Does the idea of Jesus coming alongside us as an advocate
(1 John 2:1) encourage you to conquer sin and to remain faithful?

An All-Important Question

And he asked them, "But who do you say that I am?"
Peter answered him, "You are the Christ."

MARK 8:29

Heavenly Father, of all the questions in the Bible, this is one of the most important. Who is Jesus? Everyone must respond, and the answer will mean either eternal life or death. Who do I say that Jesus is? Jesus is the Son of God—Your Son. He lived a perfect life on earth to die for humanity's sin. Without Him, I will be eternally separated from You. But by repenting of my sin and accepting Your loving gift of grace and Christ's righteousness, I am Your child, destined for heaven. May my answer to this all-important question be more than facts, Father; may it be alive in my heart, just as Your Holy Spirit is alive in my heart. Thank You for Christ. Amen.

THINK ABOUT IT:

Who do you say that Jesus is?

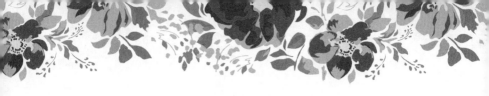

Abiding

"By this my Father is glorified, that you bear much fruit and so prove to be my disciples. As the Father has loved me, so have I loved you. Abide in my love."

JOHN 15:8-9

Heavenly Father, as Your Son, Jesus was the model of perfect obedience to You. Although I cannot expect to be perfect, I can follow in Jesus' path of obedience. I can make Your commandments the framework of my life. By living under Your commands in obedience, I place myself in the shelter of Your love, abiding there, remaining there. I can't do it alone, Father. I pray for an obedient heart. I pray for the power of the Holy Spirit to resist the temptation to follow my own path. I bow to Your wisdom in knowing what is best for me. Amen.

THINK ABOUT IT:

How can you improve your obedience to God—
and abide in His love more fully?

Divine Purpose

" 'But rise and stand upon your feet, for I have appeared to you for this purpose, to appoint you as a servant and witness. . .delivering you from your people and from the Gentiles—to whom I am sending you to open their eyes, so that they may turn from darkness to light.' "

ACTS 26:16–18

Father, when I read about Paul's conversion and calling to a life of faith, I can't help but think that this becomes the purpose of all believers. I can't help but frame these words in the context of my life. How can I be a servant to those around me, showering Your love and displaying the others-centered focus of Jesus as He walked this earth? How can I better witness to the countless lost souls, opening their eyes so they turn from darkness to the light of Your saving grace? Show me how, Father. Amen.

THINK ABOUT IT:

Have you felt called to be a servant and witness to the faith?

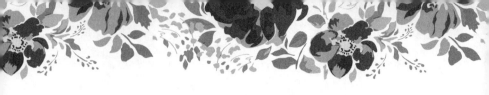

Too Deep for Words

Likewise the Spirit helps us in our weakness. For we do not know what to pray for as we ought, but the Spirit himself intercedes for us with groanings too deep for words.

ROMANS 8:26

Father, this earthly life can be overwhelming. Suffering abounds. It's hard to maintain hope of a bright future when the present seems so dismal. At times it's even difficult to put the weight of what I feel into words. But Your Holy Spirit intercedes for us. From heaven You listen, and You're faithful. Your plans will come to pass. You keep Your promises. You are good, and You desire ultimate good for Your children. Remind me of Your love, Father. When my words fail, let the groanings of the Spirit be my voice. You'll hear them loud and clear! Amen.

THINK ABOUT IT:

When prayer is a struggle, how often do you sit
in silence and let the Holy Spirit take over?

Living Temples

Or do you not know that your body is a temple of the Holy Spirit within you, whom you have from God? You are not your own, for you were bought with a price. So glorify God in your body.

1 CORINTHIANS 6:19-20

Lord, *purity* is a word teenagers usually hear a lot at church, but it is just as important as we grow into our lives as women of God. Jesus paid the ultimate price to rescue us from death. You own our bodies, Lord, and they are to be used to glorify You and to serve You. But ours is a sensual culture—much like that of the Corinthians in Paul's day. Help me make purity a priority. Purity of mind. Purity of body. Help me live counter to the culture and according to Your Word. Amen.

THINK ABOUT IT:

How can you glorify God with your purity—whether in abstinence as a single person or through faithfulness in marriage?

Lie Down and Sleep

*In peace I will both lie down and sleep; for you alone,
O LORD, make me dwell in safety.*

PSALM 4:8

Father, when I can't fall asleep, night becomes endless. My mind fills the silence with unspoken thoughts about troubles. It fills the darkness with images of an uncertain future. But it doesn't have to be like this. King David knew more chaos and danger, yet he trusted in Your care and found sleep. Nothing can happen to me that You have not foreseen; I can close my eyes and rest in Your will. When I can't fall asleep, let Your promises of love fall over me like the words of a lullaby. Let Your peace surround me like a warm blanket. You are God. You are good. I trust in Your care and find sleep. Amen.

THINK ABOUT IT:

Which verses create a sense of calm when you have trouble sleeping?

Holy Expectations

*He has told you, O man, what is good; and what does the L*ORD*
require of you but to do justice, and to love kindness,
and to walk humbly with your God?*

MICAH 6:8

Life is full of expectations, Lord. Personal expectations on who to be
and what to achieve. The expectations of others. How easy it is to feel as
though I'm not living up to expectations, especially as a Christian. Am I
enough for You, Lord? When Satan leads me to doubt myself, remind me
of Your desire for my life. You want something deeper than an outward
display of righteousness. You require a willing heart, a commitment to
do Your will. All good works flow from a heart dedicated to You. May
my expectation always be to remain humbly by Your side. Amen.

THINK ABOUT IT:

When you think about pleasing God, does your mind go
to outward behavior first or to the state of your heart?

Middle Ground

Give me neither poverty nor riches; feed me with the food that is needful for me, lest I be full and deny you and say, "Who is the LORD?" or lest I be poor and steal and profane the name of my God.

PROVERBS 30:8-9

Father, how often do I pray for just enough? Not as often as I should. While I don't pray for poverty, I have prayed for better. More. Whether more work, more friends, or more security. . .I forget that what You provide is enough. I don't desire to be in want, Father, but I also know that having more than enough can lead me to bypass the One who showers daily provision on me. Keep me humbly reliant upon Your care. Be my sufficiency. Turn this heart toward contentment in the "just enough" that You provide. Amen.

THINK ABOUT IT:

Do the words of this proverb make you
rethink your requests of God?

Counting the Cost

"For which of you, desiring to build a tower, does not first sit down and count the cost, whether he has enough to complete it?"

LUKE 14:28

Lord, thank You for the free gift of salvation! But remind me, Lord, that while salvation is through faith alone, saving faith is more than a prayer and then continuing on in the same way as before. It requires a total commitment to You—a giving up of me for Your sake. As Your disciple, I should not harbor sin—but come to You in genuine repentance. I should not cling to what this earth offers—but center my security on what You promise. I must be willing to follow where You lead. Impossible? Through my own efforts, yes; but through the sovereign work of Your Holy Spirit, I am saved! Amen.

THINK ABOUT IT:

What might discipleship cost you?

Ask for It

If any of you lacks wisdom, let him ask God, who gives generously to all without reproach, and it will be given him. But let him ask in faith, with no doubting, for the one who doubts is like a wave of the sea that is driven and tossed by the wind.

JAMES 1:5-6

Wisdom, Father, can be elusive. What is Your will for my life? How do I handle the trials this world throws at me with joy and grace? My lack of wisdom draws me ever closer to You. You have all the answers because You have written my life's story. Today I want to ask for wisdom, Father. But before I do, I need a boost in faith. In my head I say I trust You; please root out any doubt residing in my heart. Let greater wisdom begin with realizing my need for You in all things. Amen.

THINK ABOUT IT:

Do you ever find yourself asking God
for wisdom—but doubting He'll supply it?

Glory in God

But God forbid that I should glory, save in the cross of our Lord Jesus Christ, by whom the world is crucified unto me, and I unto the world.
GALATIANS 6:14 KJV

Father, it is so easy to focus on personal success, even when I'm serving You. It is so easy to rejoice in what I've done individually, what we've done as a church, when in reality all success comes from above. Keep us humble. Keep us centered on the cross. Gently remind us that success is for You, through You alone. A boost in attendance or a friend led to Jesus. Increased giving and new opportunities. In our worship services. In my path in life. For me and for my church, Father, may our successes always point to You. May I shout with joy in response to all *You've* done. Amen.

THINK ABOUT IT:

To whom is your applause directed when an individual
or your church family accomplishes something?

Spiritual Training

*Train yourself for godliness; for while bodily training is of some
value, godliness is of value in every way, as it holds promise
for the present life and also for the life to come.*

1 TIMOTHY 4:7–8

A body in motion is a good thing, Father. You designed us for movement. I want to be healthy, but I don't want to make physical fitness alone my goal. I should care for my body, while recognizing the limits. My body can only do so much. And the rewards of physical training only last on this earth, and illness and injury can quickly sweep them away. Training in Your ways provides strength and stamina to withstand the marathon of life and to serve You fully. One day this earthly body will become a heavenly body adorned with the rewards of a life lived for You. Amen.

THINK ABOUT IT:

Do you see fitness or godliness as having greater value?

Without Sight

Jesus said to him, "Have you believed because you have seen me?
Blessed are those who have not seen and yet have believed."

JOHN 20:29

Lord Jesus, we can all be Thomas at times. We ask for signs. We want proof. If only we could touch Your nail-pierced hands. . . The truth is, believing without seeing is hard. You knew this. You knew that many believers would come to faith without seeing You, the proof of Your resurrection, until heaven. So You spoke words of encouragement. By believing without seeing, I am blessed. And You have not left me without the help of Your Spirit. You "show" Yourself to me in countless ways. Through Your provision. Through Your faithful presence in my life. Through the beauty of Your creation. Through answered prayers. Lord, You are undeniable. Amen.

THINK ABOUT IT:

How do you believe without physically seeing Christ?

God the Gardener

"I am the true vine, and my Father is the vinedresser. Every branch in me that does not bear fruit he takes away, and every branch that does bear fruit he prunes, that it may bear more fruit."

JOHN 15:1-2

Father, every day is a chance to grow as a Christian and to bear fruit for You. It can be frustrating when I don't seem to make as much progress as I want to or think I should make. Remind me that You are always working, pruning me to become more like Your Son, Jesus. Often the pruning isn't pretty at first, but in time the branch will grow, the buds will appear, and my life will bear more fruit. Thank You for Your loving care, that You do not settle for what is but guide me toward fullness and beauty in You. Amen.

THINK ABOUT IT:

In what areas of your life is God the vinedresser working?

Ever the Same

Jesus Christ is the same yesterday and today and forever.
HEBREWS 13:8

Lord, change is a natural, and often necessary, part of life. From the moment of our conception, we grow. From day to day, year to year, life stage to life stage, we change. As adults, change can bring new perspectives; it can clear paths to new experiences. But also inherent in change is uncertainty. Not knowing can be scary, Father. When the changes in my life cause me to shrink back, stand close by my side. You are there even now! I can rely on Your presence and unchanging nature amid the uncertainty. Thank You for remaining constant. I don't have to wonder what Your future character will be. I already know. Amen.

THINK ABOUT IT:

Which of God's traits (His love, His faithfulness, His power, His omniscience, His goodness. . .) steady you when you face life's upheavals?

But If Not. . .

*"O Nebuchadnezzar, we have no need to answer you in this matter.
If this be so, our God whom we serve is able to deliver us from
the burning fiery furnace, and he will deliver us out of your hand,
O king. But if not, be it known to you, O king, that we will not serve
your gods or worship the golden image that you have set up."*

DANIEL 3:16-18

Father, may I have the courage of Shadrach, Meshach, and Abednego
to face the fiery trials, courage to follow Your ways and not bend to the
world's, and confidence to know that You will rescue me. And even if
You choose not to, Father, may I be committed to remain faithful as You
are faithful. Only You are holy and deserve my all. Amen.

THINK ABOUT IT:

How can being resolved to stand firm in faith
before trials help you endure them?

At Hand

The Lord is at hand; do not be anxious about anything, but in everything by prayer and supplication with thanksgiving let your requests be made known to God.

<small>PHILIPPIANS 4:5-6</small>

Father, when I am worried, I often read the words of Philippians 4:6. But as I follow Your instructions—to pray about my anxious thoughts—remind me of the words that come just before this verse: "The Lord is at hand." You are near, Father. You dwell as high as heaven, yet You are as close as my heart. As I turn my troubles over to You, may my trust grow ever stronger, rooted in Your perfect will. I will not be anxious about anything because You are here with me. Thank You for Your presence. Thank You for caring enough to listen to my prayers. Amen.

THINK ABOUT IT:

What keeps you from surrendering your anxiety fully to God?

The Walls Came Tumbling Down

By faith the walls of Jericho fell down after
they had been encircled for seven days.

HEBREWS 11:30

Lord, Your military strategy to conquer Jericho probably seemed crazy to the Israelites. But as they followed Your command and the walls fell down, they had no doubt that You were the strength behind their victory. I desire to follow Your will for my life, Lord. But when following means meeting with barriers, remind me that You are able to do wondrously more than I can imagine, even when the obstacles seem insurmountable and Your ways crazy. Your wisdom is beyond comprehension. You see the beginning and the end, and You desire only the best for me. May I trust You completely in faith. Amen.

THINK ABOUT IT:

Do you believe that God's instructions for living life and His plan for you will yield the best results—better than you can imagine?

In One Ear. . .

*But be doers of the word, and not hearers only,
deceiving yourselves. . . . The one who looks into the perfect law,
the law of liberty, and perseveres, being no hearer who forgets
but a doer who acts, he will be blessed for his doing.*

JAMES 1:22, 25

Father, as I read my Bible, I pray that the words would penetrate deeper than hearing and begin to change me. As I meditate on Your holy Word, may the truths resonate in my heart and prompt action—to conform my ways to Your ways. You offer freedom from the bondage of sin. Oh, that I would not hear the Good News and fail to thrive in total obedience to Your Word. When the Holy Spirit convicts, Father, may I be quick to respond. Your Spirit will strengthen me as I act, and through my obedience I am blessed. Amen.

THINK ABOUT IT:

How swift are you to apply the truths of God's Word to your life?

Friend of God

Whoever wishes to be a friend of the world makes himself an enemy of God. Or do you suppose it is to no purpose that the Scripture says, "He yearns jealously over the spirit that he has made to dwell in us"? But he gives more grace.

JAMES 4:4-6

Father, You held back nothing to save me. Through the blood of Your beloved Son, You made a way for me to reach You. You *want* a relationship with me. My only response should be total commitment to You. How You must feel when I choose my ways over Your ways, even for a moment! Forgive me, Father. I owe my all to You, not just the parts that are easy to surrender. Show me where I am clinging to the world and not to my faith. Pour out Your grace as I learn to humbly follow You. You are worthy of nothing less and abundantly more. Amen.

THINK ABOUT IT:

Do you see God as deserving your entire being?

Active Faith

But as for you, O man of God... Pursue righteousness, godliness,
faith, love, steadfastness, gentleness. Fight the good fight of the faith.
Take hold of the eternal life to which you were called and about which
you made the good confession in the presence of many witnesses.

1 TIMOTHY 6:11–12

Father, I love Paul's words to Timothy. The faith that he describes is not idle. It is dynamic. Timothy should *pursue, fight, take hold of....* He should not sit back and remain static in his life of faith but be actively involved in it. Father, remind me of these verses each morning. Keep me from complacency where I no longer seek to grow. May I chase after what You desire in my life. May I deepen my faith even in the darkness. May I always focus on heaven and what it means for me here on earth. Amen.

THINK ABOUT IT:

What action is God calling you to in your life?

Still Rejoice

Though the fig tree should not blossom, nor fruit be on the vines, the produce of the olive fail and the fields yield no food, the flock be cut off from the fold and there be no herd in the stalls, yet I will rejoice in the LORD; I will take joy in the God of my salvation.

HABAKKUK 3:17–18

Lord, most of us want some measure of predictability in our lives. We want the crops to yield in their time and for the harvest to be great. But prosperity is not a guarantee, and neither is a "normal" life. Hardship will happen; disruptions occur. Yet as the prophet declares, it does not need to leave us sapped of joy. You are still Lord and our salvation. We can rejoice in that fact, come what may. Amen.

THINK ABOUT IT:

Have challenging circumstances in your life
made it difficult for you to rejoice in God?

Labor Shortage

Then he said to his disciples, "The harvest is plentiful,
but the laborers are few; therefore pray earnestly to the
Lord of the harvest to send out laborers into his harvest."

MATTHEW 9:37-38

Father, there is no shortage of souls in need of Your salvation. Every human being is unrighteous apart from Christ and the cross. You rescue us from sin and welcome Your saved ones into Your family. More than that, You have made every Christian an integral part of Your plan to reconcile lives to You. What a privilege! May I be a bold witness to Your grace. And may I persistently pray for others who share the Good News. Father, You are Lord of the harvest; send out laborers that all may hear of You. Amen.

THINK ABOUT IT:

Are petitions for the spread of the Gospel
a regular part of your prayer life?

A God like No Other

Who is a God like you. . . ? He does not retain his anger forever,
because he delights in steadfast love. He will again have
compassion on us; he will tread our iniquities underfoot.
You will cast all our sins into the depths of the sea.

MICAH 7:18–19

Lord, Your love is unimaginable. That You would send Your perfect, beloved Son to die for sinners. . . That You would sacrifice so much for those who can give so little in return. . . It seems incredible. Then I read the words in Micah about Your forgiveness toward Your people, and I am even more amazed. You have compassion *again*. Your love is steadfast. Your grace is forever. Thank You. May my life be living gratitude. As I kneel before You, may I be humbled by all that You are. You are unlike any other, Lord. Amen.

THINK ABOUT IT:

What comes to mind when you consider
God's unwavering compassion toward you?

Even There

*If I take the wings of the morning and dwell in the uttermost
parts of the sea, even there your hand shall lead
me, and your right hand shall hold me.*

PSALM 139:9–10

Father, no matter where I go, You are with me. I cannot wander beyond
Your reach. I cannot stray out of Your care. You are everywhere, always,
and You are here beside me. But You are more than present. Your Word
says You lead me—guiding me in Your ways, directing me according to
Your will for my life. You hold me…drawing me to Your side, supporting
me. And when I drift, I never have far to go to return to You. You have
not abandoned me; You long for me to rest in Your presence. Thank You
for Your faithfulness. Thank You for remaining close. Amen.

THINK ABOUT IT:

Do you believe that God is present in your life even when
you have waned in your relationship with Him?

He Is Patient

But do not overlook this one fact, beloved, that with the Lord one day is as a thousand years, and a thousand years as one day. The Lord is not slow to fulfill his promise as some count slowness, but is patient toward you.

2 PETER 3:8–9

Lord, You see differently than we do. Even Your sense of time differs from ours. You have promised to return soon, but *soon* will be in Your perfect timing. In Your great love, You are patient, desiring all who will come to You to find salvation. As I wait for Christ's return, place a burden on my heart to pray for those who have not yet met You as their Lord and Savior. May I be a partner in Your waiting through prayer. Thank You for not losing Your patience toward us, Lord. Amen.

THINK ABOUT IT:

How can you best use this time to impact
the world for God's kingdom?

Let Us Rejoice

Let the heavens be glad, and let the earth rejoice; let the sea roar, and all that fills it; let the field exult, and everything in it! Then shall all the trees of the forest sing for joy before the LORD, for he comes.

PSALM 96:11–13

Lord, Your creation is marvelous. Just thinking of the vast night sky, the power of the oceans, and the beauty of the land fills my mind with wonder. But as astounding as the natural world is now, it is nothing compared with the wonder of all creation celebrating Your return. You reign, and the heavens and earth will shout before You. As Your creation—as Your child—let me shout in adoration of You. You are worthy. Fill my heart with such a deep understanding of Your greatness that I never fail to praise You. For Your might. For Your goodness. For Your grace. I worship You. Amen.

THINK ABOUT IT:

What words of praise can you bring before God today?

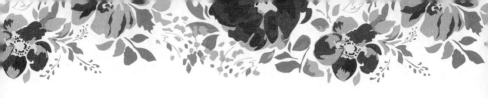

Love in Deed

*Suppose someone has enough to live and sees a brother or sister in
need, but does not help. Then God's love is not living in that person.
My children, we should love people not only with words
and talk, but by our actions and true caring.*

1 JOHN 3:17-18 NCV

Father, *loving others* is a principle I often hear in church and read in Your
Word. Loving others is what I want to do in response to Your great love
for me. But if I'm honest, it can be easier to talk about reaching out in
love than it is to actually reach out. Fear, inconvenience, selfishness...
all ugly parts of my old nature, Father, but ones You can help me
overcome. When I feel the pull of Your love to help someone, may I
respond as Your hands and feet on earth, providing out of the blessings
You have lavishly given me. Amen.

THINK ABOUT IT:

What simple or big ways can you share God's love with others?

His Word Remains

*All flesh is grass, and all its beauty is like the flower of the field.
The grass withers, the flower fades when the breath of the LORD
blows on it; surely the people are grass. The grass withers,
the flower fades, but the word of our God will stand forever.*

ISAIAH 40:6-8

Lord, a change in seasons makes the words of Isaiah so clear. Come
fall, the lush grass of summer withers and then lies dormant in winter;
next fresh spring flowers fade as summer's heat takes over. Humans
also age with time, our beauty fading. What a comfort to know that
despite the changes all creation is destined to undergo, Your Word
remains unchanged. Your plans and Your promises will not alter as the
years pass. They endure as a firm foundation to uphold Your children.
Your Word is trustworthy, Lord, and You are just as faithful. Amen.

THINK ABOUT IT:

How does the everlasting nature of God's
Word encourage you through life changes?

Be Ready

"Stay dressed for action and keep your lamps burning, and be like men who are waiting for their master to come home from the wedding feast, so that they may open the door to him at once when he comes and knocks. Blessed are those servants whom the master finds awake when he comes."

LUKE 12:35-37

Father, we women prepare many times in our lives. We get ready to go out in the morning. We schedule, plan, create. We wait for loved ones to return home. In all our busyness, let us not forget to be ready for the most important event: the return of Christ. Remind us, Father, of the words of Your Son. We should dress for action. Keep the lamps burning. Anticipate His second coming. I don't want to be idle or caught unawares on that day. Help me prepare my heart and center on You first. Amen.

THINK ABOUT IT:

Do you approach each day as if it could
be the day of Christ's return?

Totally Devoted

Do not love the world or the things in the world. . . . For all that is in the world—the desires of the flesh and the desires of the eyes and pride of life—is not from the Father but is from the world. And the world is passing away along with its desires, but whoever does the will of God abides forever.

1 JOHN 2:15-17

Lord, this world is full of distractions, distractions that Satan can use to keep me from living fully for You. From the things in the world—all the *stuff* I chase after—to the world's beliefs on how I should live, there is so much that can lead me astray. These things are not from You, Lord. And they are not here to stay. Nothing in my life should take priority over You. May I love You entirely and be devoted to You exclusively. Amen.

THINK ABOUT IT:

What does loving the world mean to you? To God?

Part of God's Family

Sing to God, sing praises to his name; lift up a song to him who rides through the deserts; his name is the LORD; exult before him! Father of the fatherless and protector of widows is God in his holy habitation. God settles the solitary in a home.

PSALM 68:4-6

God, You are almighty; You reign. You are our heavenly Father too. You care about orphans and widows. You care that Your children are in families. Whether biological, adopted, or a church family, I pray for all believers to find a place of belonging. May I reach out and be a sister to those I meet. You never meant us to live as solitary creatures. As our greatest example while He walked this earth, Your Son surrounded Himself with His disciples, a family of sorts. And He had You. I sing praises to You, my Father. Amen.

THINK ABOUT IT:

Do you need to seek out Christian brothers
and sisters to walk alongside?

Beautiful Feet

*How then will they call on him in whom they have not believed?
And how are they to believe in him of whom they have never heard?
And how are they to hear without someone preaching? And how are
they to preach unless they are sent? As it is written, "How beautiful
are the feet of those who preach the good news!"*

ROMANS 10:14-15

Lord, may I take time today, and every day, to pray for missionaries around the globe. They have accepted Your high calling to spread the Gospel. Relieve hardships, Lord. Provide out of Your boundless love. Draw hearts to You as Your disciples speak of Your salvation. Remind me too, Lord, that we are all missionaries in our own small spheres. Today, and every day, I have the chance to testify to what an amazing, eternal effect Your grace can have on an ordinary woman. Amen.

THINK ABOUT IT:

Take time this week to choose one missionary and commit
to pray for the fruitfulness of his or her work.

More Is More

But godliness with contentment is great gain, for we brought
nothing into the world, and we cannot take anything out of the world.
But if we have food and clothing, with these we will be content.

1 TIMOTHY 6:6–8

Father, with the abundance many of us enjoy, contentment should be easy. Somehow, it isn't. I lack nothing, yet so much of my time or energy goes to *things*. Contentment is a mind-set I need to cultivate daily. When I want new, better, more. . .turn my heart toward contentment, Father. Open my eyes to the overflow of material blessings I already have. Fill my days with gratitude for Your lavish provision. Lead me to share with others who don't have as much. Teach me what is sufficient and what is excess. I desire to follow Your will for my life, even in what I own. Amen.

THINK ABOUT IT:

How can turning to God first before pursuing
more keep you focused on contentment?

For One

"What man of you, having a hundred sheep, if he has lost one of them, does not leave the ninety-nine in the open country, and go after the one that is lost, until he finds it? And when he has found it, he lays it on his shoulders, rejoicing. . . . Just so, I tell you, there will be more joy in heaven over one sinner who repents than over ninety-nine righteous persons who need no repentance."

LUKE 15:4–5, 7

Lord, what a beautiful picture of salvation! You, the Great Shepherd, seek the lost—not only for a time, but until You find us. And then You bring the lost ones back to Your flock. You rejoice over our return. May our response be joy too and not pride like the religious leaders of Jesus' day. We need Your guiding hand to bring us back to You. Lead us. Save us. Thank You for Your care. Amen.

THINK ABOUT IT:

How have you seen the Great Shepherd work in your life?

Ready and Willing

And the angel answered her, ". . .nothing will be impossible with God." And Mary said, "Behold, I am the servant of the Lord; let it be to me according to your word."

LUKE 1:35, 37-38

Father, what went through Mary's mind when she heard the angel's news that day, and then when she faced a radically changed life—one she would never have imagined—all the days that followed? Confusion? Fear? Dread? Joy? Your plans don't always make sense to Your children, Father. I want to learn from Mary. Whatever emotions she felt, she trusted You. She humbly submitted to Your will. You may ask me to do difficult things in my life, things that seem impossible. When doubt creeps in, remind me that nothing is impossible for You. You have great plans for me—ones I would never imagine apart from You. Ones I will accept with open arms. Amen.

THINK ABOUT IT:

When God leads you in an unexpected
direction, what is your response?

Blessed Are. . .

"Blessed are the poor in spirit, for theirs is the kingdom of heaven. Blessed are those who mourn, for they shall be comforted. Blessed are the meek, for they shall inherit the earth. Blessed are those who hunger and thirst for righteousness, for they shall be satisfied. Blessed are the merciful, for they shall receive mercy. Blessed are the pure in heart, for they shall see God."

MATTHEW 5:3-8

Perhaps it is part of our culture, Lord, but the idea of "being blessed" often equals material or transitory things of this world. We are blessed with comfortable homes, full pantries, expendable income, beauty, health. . . What You consider "blessed," though, goes much deeper than the physical. You shower us with so many intangible things, including relationship with You. Widen my perspective on blessing, Lord. I am blessed indeed! Amen.

THINK ABOUT IT:

What are the many ways God shows you blessing?

Just Pray

"And when you pray, don't be like those people who don't know God. They continue saying things that mean nothing, thinking that God will hear them because of their many words. Don't be like them, because your Father knows the things you need before you ask him."

MATTHEW 6:7-8 NCV

God, as I kneel before You in prayer, keep my words simple. May each one have meaning and not be empty words, empty phrases. I don't need to fill Your ears with endless talk for You to hear, because You have promised to listen to me when I pray to You in faith. You are my heavenly Father; You want me to come to You as Your child. I'm calling out to You today, in reverence but also with assurance that my Abba hears me and knows what I need even before I form the words on my tongue. Amen.

THINK ABOUT IT:

Do memorized prayers come easier to you than pleas to God as a child to her Father?

The Joy of the Lord

Then he said to them, "Go your way. Eat the fat and drink
sweet wine and send portions to anyone who has nothing
ready, for this day is holy to our Lord. And do not be
grieved, for the joy of the LORD is your strength."

NEHEMIAH 8:10

Lord, the nation of Judah had been through years of captivity and struggle and sin, yet they still had reason to celebrate. The joy of the Lord—their God, You—was their strength. For me too there is reason to celebrate, even in difficult times, because of Your presence in my life. I can experience joy to do life's hard tasks, life's mundane tasks, life's impossible tasks, because You are with me. You strengthen me. No matter what, I have Your gift of grace, and that alone is reason to rejoice. Amen.

THINK ABOUT IT:

What ways can you acknowledge and celebrate
God's strengthening in your life?

Living Sacrifices

*So brothers and sisters, since God has shown us great mercy, I beg you
to offer your lives as a living sacrifice to him. . . . Be changed within
by a new way of thinking. Then you will be able to decide
what God wants for you; you will know what is good
and pleasing to him and what is perfect.*

ROMANS 12:1–2 NCV

Lord, with the sacrifice of Your Son on the cross, we believers no longer need to offer animal sacrifices to You. The shed blood of the Lamb saves us. In response, I can offer my life as a living sacrifice. All that I do becomes worship and service to You. But doing so requires guidance, Lord. As I read and meditate on scripture, Your Holy Spirit will change me from the inside. I will see Your will for me, and my life will be a daily reflection of Your grace. Amen.

THINK ABOUT IT:

What comes to mind when you think of
your life as a living sacrifice?

Day by Day

*So we do not lose heart. Though our outer self is wasting away,
our inner self is being renewed day by day. For this light
momentary affliction is preparing for us an eternal weight
of glory beyond all comparison, as we look not to the
things that are seen but to the things that are unseen.*

2 Corinthians 4:16–18

Father, our earthly bodies are not eternal bodies. Illness, fatigue, injury, aging. . .we are fragile creatures! Some days—when I am healthy—it's easy to ignore this truth. But when I am weak, I must turn to You. As I admit my weakness, though, the words of Paul remind me that I should not lose heart. You renew me day in, day out. You are making me strong for my forever home in heaven. Once I am there, Your glory will outshine any darkness I experience in this life. Amen.

THINK ABOUT IT:

How can you look at whatever afflicts you today
or tomorrow through God's eyes?

What's On Your Mind?

Finally, brethren, whatsoever things are true, whatsoever things
are honest, whatsoever things are just, whatsoever things are pure,
whatsoever things are lovely, whatsoever things are of good report;
if there be any virtue, and if there be any praise, think on these things.

PHILIPPIANS 4:8 KJV

Father, as a woman, I tend to think a lot. I mentally list the tasks I have to accomplish on any given day and then feel the pressure of getting everything done. I worry about family, friends. I contemplate what I did, or should have done, in the past and what awaits me in the future. I labor over all that is going wrong in the world. . . . Please stop my churning thoughts, Father. Remind me of the things You would have me dwell on—things that are true, honest, just, pure, lovely. Positive things. Things worthy of praise. Refresh my mind today. Amen.

THINK ABOUT IT:
How can you begin to replace negative ways of thinking
with God's prescription for your mind?

One of a Kind Creation

Make a careful exploration of who you are and the work you have been given, and then sink yourself into that. Don't be impressed with yourself. Don't compare yourself with others. Each of you must take responsibility for doing the creative best you can with your own life.

GALATIANS 6:4-5 MSG

Father, You lovingly created me as an individual. From the way I look to who I am to what I do—my entire being is the work of Your hands. As I take on this life You've given me, keep me humble and focused on what You do *through* me. Guard my heart against comparison, Father. With the bombardment of social media, seeing what others are doing is the new normal. May I be bold to step away from that norm so I fulfill my calling and do not yearn for someone else's. Amen.

THINK ABOUT IT:

Have you taken time to discover who
you—God's unique creation—are?

Hope Is. . .

For in this hope we were saved. Now hope that is seen is not hope.
For who hopes for what he sees? But if we hope for what
we do not see, we wait for it with patience.

ROMANS 8:24-25

Lord, humans can hope for many things, and hope can mean many things. As a Christian, I find my hope in You. Hope gives me reason to face the day ahead. Hope says that despite the bad, good will ultimately triumph. Hope lifts me from the depths to heaven's heights. And even though I can't see what I hope for yet, it is certain. I don't have to hope in *maybe*; I hope in what is sure to come. My eternity is secure with You, and one day I will share in Your glory. Thank You for not leaving us without hope, Lord. Amen.

THINK ABOUT IT:
How does knowing that your future is safe with
God change your definition of *hope*?

Search Me!

Search me, O God, and know my heart! Try me and know my
thoughts! And see if there be any grievous way in me,
and lead me in the way everlasting!

PSALM 139:23-24

God, in the moment I chose to accept Jesus Christ as my Savior and Lord, I was saved. With nothing to offer in return, I became a child of God. But my life as Your daughter does not end at salvation. You want to transform me, to mold me. On my own, I could never change, so I invite You, just as David did, to search me. Know my heart, God. Test me and my thoughts. Root out any sinful tendencies, and guide me in the path of righteousness paid for by Jesus. May I always welcome Your tender leading in my life. Amen.

THINK ABOUT IT:

Is the thought of God probing you scary or comforting?

Press On!

Brothers and sisters, I know that I have not yet reached that goal, but there is one thing I always do. Forgetting the past and straining toward what is ahead, I keep trying to reach the goal and get the prize for which God called me through Christ to the life above.

PHILIPPIANS 3:13–14 NCV

Father, as I move toward my goal of Christlike-ness, remind me that the Christian life is more marathon than sprint. I will not reach perfection on this earth. At times I will feel as though I'm bolting full speed ahead; at others I may be crawling inch by inch. I'll have triumphs, and I'll make mistakes. In each of these moments, help me focus on You alone, not being burdened by the past but looking forward to the prize of complete Christlike-ness in my eternal home. Amen.

THINK ABOUT IT:

How does the promise of heaven encourage you to persevere in both the successes and stumbles of your Christian journey?

Eternal Joy

"When a woman is giving birth, she has sorrow because her hour has come, but when she has delivered the baby, she no longer remembers the anguish, for joy that a human being has been born into the world. So also you have sorrow now, but I will see you again, and your hearts will rejoice, and no one will take your joy from you."

JOHN 16:21-22

Lord, Your crucifixion must have been a sorrowful time indeed for Your disciples. But You reminded them of the joy that would follow the anguish. Although You would see them again physically—after Your resurrection—You also left them with the promise of Your Holy Spirit. Their hearts would "see" You forever and rejoice. I share in that same joy. Despite the sorrowful circumstances of this life, Your Spirit is with me permanently, and that is cause for rejoicing. Thank You for being my joy. Amen.

THINK ABOUT IT:

Do you believe that the joy of knowing Christ
can overshadow any sorrow in this life?

For God's Sake

Be subject for the Lord's sake to every human institution. . . .
For this is the will of God, that by doing good you should
put to silence the ignorance of foolish people.

1 PETER 2:13, 15

It's true, God, if you want to start an argument, bring up religion or politics. More and more, the political world alone seems to be in upheaval. Once united, many are divided over policies. While I'm not to obey when any government tells me to act against Your laws, as a Christian, I should submit to the laws of my country and respect the leaders of this land. My good conduct does not open a door for unbelievers to attack the faith. I want to bring honor to You, God. Submission is one way I can reveal what it means to be Your child. Amen.

THINK ABOUT IT:

Before you speak or act regarding politics, do you pause
first to consider how it will reflect on God?

Worthy Women

"Many women have done excellently, but you surpass them all."
Charm is deceitful, and beauty is vain, but a woman who fears
the LORD is to be praised. Give her of the fruit of he
hands, and let her works praise her in the gates.
PROVERBS 31:29–31

Lord, how can we as women not be intimidated by the unnamed woman of Proverbs 31? We read of her and begin the mental checklist of all the ways we don't measure up. I have to believe that making women the world over feel inadequate is not Your purpose for these verses, Lord. If I focus less on what she does specifically and more on what she values, I can learn from her; I can grow as a woman of God. Her actions speak of resourcefulness, initiative, generosity, self-respect, faith, and more… all qualities I can embody in my own way. Show me how, Lord. May I be worthy of praise. Amen.

THINK ABOUT IT:

What ways are you a Proverbs 31 woman?

Love Eternal

For I am persuaded, that neither death, nor life, nor angels,
nor principalities, nor powers, nor things present, nor things to come,
nor height, nor depth, nor any other creature, shall be able to separate
us from the love of God, which is in Christ Jesus our Lord.

ROMANS 8:38-39 KJV

Lord, that You love me is amazing. You are almighty God. You reign over earth and the heavens; You created the universe! And yet You desire relationship with me—one human among countless others. Your love is immense. . .and it is everlasting. Nothing in this world or out of this world, now or ever, will keep Your love from me. When all else in life seems to disintegrate, I know the love of God will hold me unwaveringly. Words are never enough, Lord, but let me thank You for Your love. Amen.

THINK ABOUT IT:

If love is the greatest power on earth,
how much greater is God's love for us?

Like Honey to the Soul

My son, eat honey, for it is good, and the drippings of the honeycomb are sweet to your taste. Know that wisdom is such to your soul; if you find it, there will be a future, and your hope will not be cut off.

PROVERBS 24:13-14

Father, it is easy to think of "wisdom" as dry—something acquired with age. But the scriptures declare wisdom to be sweet—something to be sought even in youth. Wisdom goes deep into our lives and enriches our souls. Wisdom is the nectar we need to thrive. Help me find wisdom, Father. May I daily go to the source of wisdom, Your Word, in search of the insights that bring a future and hope. Whisper to my heart so that I may know You and Your will more fully, so that I may grow in understanding. Amen.

THINK ABOUT IT:

What rewards does wisdom bring to the believer's life?

For My Good

*For I know the plans I have for you, declares the L*ORD*, plans for welfare and not for evil, to give you a future and a hope.*

JEREMIAH 29:11

When circumstances in my world overwhelm me, Father, when I can't see my way out of another day, it is hard to trust in the goodness of Your plans. Maybe I find it difficult to see the good, the future, the hope because my focus is off. You see from above, a heavenly point of view. My view is so very limited. Help me see through Your eyes. You envision my life, and You want more than happiness; You want joy. You want more than "getting by"; You want abundance. You want the peace and security that only come from utter dependence on You. When my world crumbles, shift my focus, Father. Amen.

THINK ABOUT IT:

How will aligning your perspective on life with God's help allow you to rest in His sovereign care?

A Checklist for Love

Love is patient and kind; love does not envy or boast; it is not arrogant or rude. It does not insist on its own way; it is not irritable or resentful; it does not rejoice at wrongdoing, but rejoices with the truth. Love bears all things, believes all things, hopes all things, endures all things.

1 CORINTHIANS 13:4-7

God, love is so central in Your Word. You loved us, so You sent Your Son. We are to love You and love others. As I live a life of love, may the words in 1 Corinthians be my guide. May my love be patient and kind, content with my lot, happy for others, and humble. May it be mindful of others and not always seeking my own benefit, long-suffering and able to let go of grudges while holding on to and celebrating truth. May it bear all, believe all, hope, and endure. Amen.

THINK ABOUT IT:

What does lived out love look like?

Palms Heavenward

*Humble yourselves, therefore, under the mighty hand of God
so that at the proper time he may exalt you, casting all
your anxieties on him, because he cares for you.*

1 PETER 5:6-7

Lord, as I pray today, the cares of this world distract me. My mind wanders from praise and prayer to all the things left undone, to all the problems and concerns in my life right now. So I kneel before You with open hands, palms toward the sky. I let go of every thought that keeps me from precious communion with You. Where I am weak, You are more than capable of shouldering these burdens. I come to You humbly, submitting to Your omniscience and timing in caring for me. I believe You will exalt me above these difficult circumstances how and when You see fit. I release them to You, Lord. Amen.

THINK ABOUT IT:

What keeps you from handing over your cares to God?

Order My Steps

The heart of man plans his way,
but the LORD establishes his steps.

PROVERBS 16:9

Father, most of us do some planning in our lives. We make business plans, life plans, vacation plans, meal plans. Planning is useful, often necessary. Yet I can plan and plan and plan, then even the smallest thing gone wrong reminds me that, ultimately, I am not in control. This can send me into a panic, or it can push me toward You. While I am not in control, Father, You are! Always. I cannot see all the curves ahead, let alone around them, but You can. I cannot remain strong through the ups and downs, but You can hold me steady. When I don't know whether to turn left or right, You guide me. You establish my steps. Amen.

THINK ABOUT IT:

What planning in your life do you need to surrender
to God before taking your first step?

No Eye Has Seen. . .

But, as it is written, "What no eye has seen, nor ear heard, nor the heart of man imagined, what God has prepared for those who love him"—these things God has revealed to us through the Spirit. For the Spirit searches everything, even the depths of God.

1 CORINTHIANS 2:9–10

God, Your truth is deep, Your wisdom immense. We cannot obtain it like ordinary truth and wisdom—by eyes and ears and mind. The Holy Spirit must reveal it. Open me to Your truth, in Your Word and as Your Spirit whispers to my heart. I need Your wisdom guiding me through this life, step by step, moment by moment. Where my understanding is so limited, Yours is unimaginable. But You reveal Your wisdom to the ones You love. Reveal it to me, I pray. Amen.

THINK ABOUT IT:

Is it easy to wait for the revealed wisdom of the Holy Spirit, or do you find yourself relying on the "wisdom of this age"(1 Corinthians 2:6)?

With One Voice

*May the God of endurance and encouragement grant you to live
in such harmony with one another, in accord with Christ Jesus,
that together you may with one voice glorify the God
and Father of our Lord Jesus Christ.*

Romans 15:5-6

Father, Your children are part of Your family, united through the blood of Your Son. At times, like our earthly families, we argue. Where Your Word is silent on some issues, we have an opinion. We want to have our say—whether we speak softly in our small circles or shout loudly to the whole congregation. But Your desire is harmony, not discord. So we cry out with the apostle Paul, Father, that You grant us the endurance and encouragement we need to live in harmony. Our goal? To speak together of Your glory. Amen.

THINK ABOUT IT:
Where can you be a voice of unity in your church family?

Not What You'd Expect

But God chose what is foolish in the world to shame the wise; God chose what is weak in the world to shame the strong; God chose what is low and despised in the world, even things that are not, to bring to nothing things that are, so that no human being might boast in the presence of God.

1 CORINTHIANS 1:27-29

Lord, Your ways are higher than ours (Isaiah 55:9). And they are often the opposite. Where we would choose the beautiful, the powerful, the popular, You choose the plain, the lowly, the underdog. A baby born to be a Savior. The weak become strong. Humble ones inherit the kingdom. Sinners find forgiveness. All the glory belongs to You, Lord, for without You we are nothing. Through You, we are children of the Most High. Amen.

THINK ABOUT IT:

When was the last time you were surprised
by the amazing ways God works?

An Empathetic Savior

For we do not have a high priest who is unable to sympathize with
our weaknesses, but one who in every respect has been tempted
as we are, yet without sin. Let us then with confidence draw
near to the throne of grace, that we may receive
mercy and find grace to help in time of need.

HEBREWS 4:15–16

Lord Jesus, You walked the earth as I do. You've known pain, hunger, weariness, emotion. You faced temptation in the wilderness for forty days and forty nights. There is nothing I can go through that You don't understand. Yet, unlike me, You are blameless. It is only through Your sinless life that I gain life eternal. I can come boldly to the throne seeking forgiveness, seeking grace, knowing that I will find an advocate in You. Help me walk this earth as You did. Amen.

THINK ABOUT IT:

When you are in life's wilderness, do you have confidence
to approach Christ for the grace you need?

With Equal Measure

The point is this: whoever sows sparingly will also reap sparingly, and whoever sows bountifully will also reap bountifully. Each one must give as he has decided in his heart, not reluctantly or under compulsion, for God loves a cheerful giver.

2 CORINTHIANS 9:6–7

God, You have given me so much. You gave Your Son for my redemption. You fill my life with Your blessings. I thank You for Your overwhelming generosity toward me. As I budget, help me give out of such a generous heart. Open my eyes to see the good that comes from pouring Your resources into others. And just as You give out of love, may my giving flow from love, not with a sense of obligation but with joy in witnessing Your hand at work. The blessings will be plentiful. Amen.

THINK ABOUT IT:

Do you believe that God will pour into
your life as much as you pour out?

Anchored

So when God desired to show more convincingly to the heirs of the
promise the unchangeable character of his purpose, he guaranteed
it with an oath, so that by two unchangeable things, in which it is
impossible for God to lie, we who have fled for refuge might have
strong encouragement to hold fast to the hope set before us.
We have this as a sure and steadfast anchor of the soul.

HEBREWS 6:17–19

God, when You make a promise, You keep it. Unlike people, who have let me down, You are faithful. I do not have to wonder if what You said is true. You, almighty God who cannot lie, guarantee that it is. I can run to Your promises as refuge; I can rest in Your promises as an anchor for my soul. May I never waver in my trust, I pray. Amen.

THINK ABOUT IT:

What truths from God's Word help you when
you begin to doubt His promises?

Content No Matter What

I have learned in whatever situation I am to be content. I know how to be brought low, and I know how to abound. In any and every circumstance, I have learned the secret of facing plenty and hunger, abundance and need. I can do all things through him who strengthens me.

PHILIPPIANS 4:11-13

Lord, there's no telling what this life will bring. Much like what Paul described, I will experience good times and bad, be brought low and abound, face plenty and need. But whatever my current state or the future holds, I know the key to living successfully in contentment— total reliance on You. It is not only in the difficult times that I need You, Lord. I need You every day, good or bad. You strengthen me to live according to Your will, come what may. Amen.

THINK ABOUT IT:

How is Christ strengthening you to face today?

If Only

*And behold, a woman who had suffered from a discharge of blood
for twelve years came up behind him and touched the fringe of
his garment, for she said to herself, "If I only touch his garment,
I will be made well." Jesus turned, and seeing her he said,
"Take heart, daughter; your faith has made you well."*

MATTHEW 9:20-22

Oh, to have the faith of this woman! Lord, she believed that Your power
was so great that even touching the fringe of Your clothes would heal
her. And she was right; You are almighty. As I face the difficult times in
my life, remind me that You are able to heal, to save, with just a word.
So much of the fear and doubt I experience comes from a faulty view
of You. What appears impossible is possible under Your mighty hand.
May I never limit my faith by underestimating You, Lord. Amen.

THINK ABOUT IT:

How does an inadequate conception of God
keep you from living fully in faith?

Ready to Hear

*And the Lord came and stood, calling as at other times,
"Samuel! Samuel!" And Samuel said, "Speak,
for your servant hears."*

1 SAMUEL 3:10

Lord, four times You called Samuel. You didn't stop when he didn't hear *You*. You called again. And You kept calling until he understood. Then Samuel was ready to listen, ready to obey. Throughout my life, You call to me. Sometimes I'm slow to hear, or I think I hear and then act when I really don't understand yet. Be patient with me, I pray. As I hurry to do what's in my mind, draw me back to You, to a place where I can listen for Your voice. Never give up calling my name until I hear—really hear—and obey. I want to be a willing servant, ready to follow Your leading. Amen.

THINK ABOUT IT:

Do you pause in your prayers to leave space
for the Holy Spirit to "call" to your heart?

Light Up the World

Do all things without grumbling or disputing, that you may be
blameless and innocent, children of God without blemish in the
midst of a crooked and twisted generation, among whom you
shine as lights in the world, holding fast to the word of life.

PHILIPPIANS 2:14–16

Father, may I be ever mindful of the impression I leave with others about my faith. If I am downcast and complaining about Your will in my life, how will others see Your loving care despite difficult times? If I constantly question Your sovereignty, who will turn to You as Lord? I want to reflect Your love, the joy of being Your child, and the peace that only flows from You. As I shine as a light in the darkness, let others see and draw close to life. Amen.

THINK ABOUT IT:

How do others see Christ and a life of faith when they look at you?

Our Deliverance

For we were so utterly burdened beyond our strength that we despaired of life itself. . . . But that was to make us rely not on ourselves but on God who raises the dead. He delivered us from such a deadly peril, and he will deliver us. On him we have set our hope that he will deliver us again. You also must help us by prayer.

2 CORINTHIANS 1:8–11

Father, Your children face many difficult, sometimes frightening, times. Natural disasters, terrorism, persecution. . . In those times, You are our hope and rescue. You have the power to deliver us—from danger, evil, even death. As we face what seem to be insurmountable circumstances, guard our hearts. Draw us close so that we depend only on You. Remind us also to pray for those who are burdened beyond what they are able to bear alone. May they find relief in relying on Your strength. Amen.

THINK ABOUT IT:

Do you believe God can use despair to deepen our faith?

Free in Christ

*For freedom Christ has set us free; stand firm therefore, and do
not submit again to a yoke of slavery.... You were running
well. Who hindered you from obeying the truth?
This persuasion is not from him who calls you.*

GALATIANS 5:1, 7–8

Lord, believers in the early church encountered those who added
works to grace. While good flows from a heart of faith, it is not
what grants salvation. Christ sets us free. The grace that brings
redemption allows us to live lives unburdened by guilt over past
sin and strengthened through the Holy Spirit to reject present sin.
May I never be led astray from a life rooted in faith alone, Lord. May
I be free from the shackles of legalism and sin, and free to live for
You. Amen.

THINK ABOUT IT:

What burdens of legalism are keeping you
from thriving under God's grace?

Direct from God

All Scripture is breathed out by God and profitable for teaching, for reproof, for correction, and for training in righteousness, that the man of God may be complete, equipped for every good work.

2 TIMOTHY 3:16-17

Lord, Your Word is amazing! It is a part of You, Your very breath, and through it You speak softly to my heart. You did not leave me to try and learn Your righteous ways on my own; that would be impossible for me. So You left Your Word, holy and unchanged through history, to reveal Your truth. With it You convict me of sin and point me toward repentance and healing. Your sweet words buoy me in difficulty. They lead me back to You when I stray. They whisper wisdom in times of greatest need. What can Your Word not do? Amen.

THINK ABOUT IT:

Do you approach reading the Bible as a chore or as a chance to hear God speak into your life?

Death Vanquished

"Death is swallowed up in victory." "O death, where is your victory?
O death, where is your sting?" The sting of death is sin,
and the power of sin is the law. But thanks be to God,
who gives us the victory through our Lord Jesus Christ.

1 CORINTHIANS 15:54–57

Father, nothing on this earth strikes quite as much fear as death. Even the thought of it is like a painful sting. Death, spiritual and physical, is what every person faces—apart from You. When You sent Your precious, perfect Son to die in our place, You broke the power of death. You provided a way to righteousness, a way to life with You. Even in the pain of this world, we have victory. We need not fear but can hold on to hope of eternity with You in heaven. Thank You, Father! Amen.

THINK ABOUT IT:

How does your view of death change when you focus on Jesus?

Praise Him

Blessed be the name of the Lord from this time forth and forevermore! From the rising of the sun to its setting, the name of the Lord is to be praised! The Lord is high above all nations, and his glory above the heavens! Who is like the Lord our God, who is seated on high, who looks far down on the heavens and the earth?

PSALM 113:2–6

God, You are like no other. In this world or out of it, You are high above all. As I come to You in prayer, may my first thoughts be praise to You, for everything You do, for everything You are. Forever. So many times my focus is on me when I should lift my eyes to You and raise my hands in worship. Blessed is Your name, God. Worthy are You of my praise. Amen.

THINK ABOUT IT:

How can you make praise a daily part of your prayers and your life?

Joy Just Ahead

Weeping may tarry for the night, but joy comes with the morning. . . .
You have turned for me my mourning into dancing; you have loosed
my sackcloth and clothed me with gladness, that my glory
may sing your praise and not be silent. O LORD
my God, I will give thanks to you forever!

PSALM 30:5, 11–12

Father, we all face dark nights in this life. Whether financial strain, sickness, or the loss of a loved one, hard times can sap our energy and leave us weeping. When I face difficulty, be with me to dry my tears. Hold me tight until the morning dawns. Then I will dance with joy. I will sing of Your power to transform me, to transform what once seemed an endless darkness into bright glory. I cry out with David: my God, I will give thanks to You forever! Amen.

THINK ABOUT IT:

How has your faith helped you endure trying
times with the hope of joy to come?

Thirsty for the Word

*So put away all malice and all deceit and hypocrisy and
envy and all slander. Like newborn infants, long for the pure
spiritual milk, that by it you may grow up into salvation—
if indeed you have tasted that the Lord is good.*

1 PETER 2:1-3

Father, when I first came to You, I was like an infant, and like an infant who grows day by day, I am to grow in my faith. But spiritual growth can't happen if I'm harboring sin. Help me clear sin from my life and instead thirst for Your Word. Like milk for my soul, it has all that I need to mature in my Christian walk. You are good, Father, and Your goodness toward me propels me to seek Your truth. May I never stop growing. Amen.

THINK ABOUT IT:
Do you long for the spiritual milk of God's Word,
or do you need to pray for renewed thirst?

Holy Correction

For the moment all discipline seems painful rather than pleasant, but later it yields the peaceful fruit of righteousness to those who have been trained by it. Therefore lift your drooping hands and strengthen your weak knees, and make straight paths for your feet, so that what is lame may not be put out of joint but rather be healed.

HEBREWS 12:11–13

Heavenly Father, when a loving parent disciplines a child, it is for the child's good, to teach her and keep her safe. You do the same for Your children, for me. You guide me toward holiness; You keep me from harm. While the discipline is unpleasant, it flows from Your immense love. I don't want to become discouraged or bitter—but to yield, opening my eyes and ears to what You would have me learn. You see the end result: a healed me. Amen.

THINK ABOUT IT:

Would God's love for us be complete
without His divine discipline?

Jesus, Most High

*He is the image of the invisible God, the firstborn of all creation.
For by him all things were created, in heaven and on earth, visible and
invisible, whether thrones or dominions or rulers or authorities—
all things were created through him and for him. And he is
before all things, and in him all things hold together.*

COLOSSIANS 1:15-17

Jesus, may I never forget the miracle that You are—God in flesh. In every attribute You are creator God, yet You walked the earth side by side with Your creation. You are above all, yet You humbled Yourself to seek lost souls and bring them to Your throne of grace. As one of Your created beings, I exist to give You glory. I praise You for holding everything together—from the vast universe to my individual life. Amen.

THINK ABOUT IT:
In seeing Christ as a baby born and a man crucified,
do you worship Him also as holy God?

Loyal Woman

*But Ruth said, "Do not urge me to leave you or to return from following
you. For where you go I will go, and where you lodge I will lodge.
Your people shall be my people, and your God my God."*

RUTH 1:16

God, You prize loyalty; You honor it. Ruth, burdened by the grief over
losing her husband, could have sought solace by returning to her
homeland, her people. But Ruth knew where she belonged—beside
Naomi. She knew her role—to offer support to her family and worship to
You. Despite the prospect of difficult times ahead, Ruth remained loyal,
and You rewarded that loyalty. May my life display such faithfulness,
God. May I never abandon my loved ones or You for the safe path.
However rocky or clear the road ahead may be, You, ever loyal, will
remain by my side. Amen.

THINK ABOUT IT:

What blessings might Ruth have lost had
she chosen comfort over faith?

Every Need

Then Jesus called his disciples to him and said, "I have compassion
on the crowd because they have been with me now three days
and have nothing to eat. And I am unwilling to send
them away hungry, lest they faint on the way."

MATTHEW 15:32

Jesus, while You lived on earth, You did many amazing acts. You healed the sick and cast out demons. You walked on water and calmed storms. You lived a sinless life to rescue a sinful world. Along with all the miraculous, You were still Lord of the everyday too. You knew the crowd gathered to hear You would be hungry; You had compassion and provided for their need. Still today, You know what I need. You anticipate my weakness and have a plan to see me through. You watch out for me when I can't see the trouble ahead. Thank You for Your compassion for even the smallest care. Amen.

THINK ABOUT IT:

Why has God preserved these words of Jesus for us to read today?

Pay Attention

Therefore we must pay much closer attention to what we have heard,
lest we drift away from it. For since the message declared by angels
proved to be reliable, and every transgression or disobedience
received a just retribution, how shall we escape if we neglect such
a great salvation? It was declared at first by the Lord,
and it was attested to us by those who heard.

HEBREWS 2:1–3

Lord, Your Gospel is an anchor for our lives. It is the truth that saves, proven without doubt over the centuries. The writer of Hebrews warns us to pay attention—close attention—to what we've heard. We are not to hear and move on but we are to make the message the center of us. Impress on me the importance of Your words, Lord, that I may remain close, anchored to Your salvation as the direction for my life. Amen.

THINK ABOUT IT:

Do you need to re-center the Gospel message in your life?

For Eternity

Of old you laid the foundation of the earth, and the heavens are the work of your hands. They will perish, but you will remain; they will all wear out like a garment. You will change them like a robe, and they will pass away, but you are the same, and your years have no end.

PSALM 102:25-27

Lord, just looking through my closet, I can see the truth of this psalm. No matter how well made and beautiful they were when new, clothes wear out. The seams weaken; the fabric thins and tears over time. Eventually I toss them away. Your creation is just the same. No matter how well made and beautiful it may have been when You spoke it into existence, this earth and all in it will come to an end. But You remain eternal, God. Praise to You forever. Amen.

THINK ABOUT IT:

Because change is such a normal part of this life,
is it difficult to see God as unchanging?

Help or Hinder

From that time Jesus began to show his disciples that he must go to Jerusalem and suffer many things. . . . And Peter took him aside and began to rebuke him, saying, "Far be it from you, Lord! This shall never happen to you." But he turned and said to Peter, "Get behind me, Satan! You are a hindrance to me. For you are not setting your mind on the things of God, but on the things of man."

Lord, You loved Peter. He was one of Your trusted disciples and a part of building the early church. But he was human and susceptible to Satan's schemes. Anyone and anything not in line with Your divine plan is a hindrance. I don't want to get in Your way, Lord. I want to be a part of forwarding Your plans—in my life and the world. Shift my thoughts toward You, I pray. Amen.

THINK ABOUT IT:

Is your mind-set making you a stumbling block
or a stepping-stone in God's plan?

Approach in Faith

But she came and knelt before him, saying, "Lord, help me." And he answered, "It is not right to take the children's bread and throw it to the dogs." She said, "Yes, Lord, yet even the dogs eat the crumbs that fall from their masters' table." Then Jesus answered her, "O woman, great is your faith! Be it done for you as you desire."

MATTHEW 15:25-28

Lord, Your message was first for Israel, Your covenant people. But that did not stop this Canaanite woman from seeking You. She approached You with great faith, determined to receive even a scrap of blessing from You, knowing it would be more than enough. Persistence and confidence paid off. May I approach You in prayer with such persistence and confidence, knowing that You are able to do the miraculous. You respond to humble expressions of faith, Lord. Hear my cry today. Amen.

THINK ABOUT IT:

Do you approach God with faith that He will answer?

Our Good Shepherd

"The sheep hear his voice, and he calls his own sheep by name and leads them out. When he has brought out all his own, he goes before them, and the sheep follow him, for they know his voice. . . . I am the good shepherd. The good shepherd lays down his life for the sheep."

JOHN 10:3-4, 11

Lord, what a beautiful picture of how You care for us! You call to us—Your own sheep—by name and lead us, as a personal, caring shepherd. You go before us, showing us the way to take. And in the ultimate expression of Your love, You laid down Your life that we might live. As one of Your sheep, I know Your voice when You call. Call to me now so that I follow You and learn from Your way. Amen.

THINK ABOUT IT:

What does Jesus' name of Good Shepherd mean to you?

Self-Denial

"If anyone would come after me, let him deny himself and take up his cross and follow me. For whoever would save his life will lose it, but whoever loses his life for my sake and the gospel's will save it. For what does it profit a man to gain the whole world and forfeit his soul?"

MARK 8:34-36

Lord, as a follower of You, my life will not look like a nonbeliever's. What I chase after, what I model my ways after, will be different. Following You means sacrifice, just as salvation meant Your sacrifice on the cross. The sacrifice is not in vain! I can spend my energy, my time, my resources— my life—seeking to gain comfort and security and happiness in this world; but when death comes, it will amount to nothing. If, instead, I spend my energy, my time, my resources—my all—for Your sake, I will gain so much more. Amen.

THINK ABOUT IT:

What does "denying self" look like in your life?

The Green God

"How difficult it will be for those who have wealth to enter the kingdom of God!" And the disciples were amazed at his words. But Jesus said to them again, "Children, how difficult it is to enter the kingdom of God! It is easier for a camel to go through the eye of a needle than for a rich person to enter the kingdom of God."

MARK 10:23-25

Money. God, why is it so important to us? We idolize it. We pursue it. We hoard it, protect it, invest it, dream about what we can do with it. If only we had enough money. . . We would be no better off than if we were paupers apart from You. Nothing in this world can secure what we need most—salvation. The riches of eternity begin and end in You. May I loosen my hold on money, God, and cling to You instead. Amen.

THINK ABOUT IT:

Why does the "security" of money keep
people from turning to God?

Missing the Point

"O you of little faith, why are you discussing among yourselves the fact that you have no bread? Do you not yet perceive? Do you not remember the five loaves for the five thousand, and how many baskets you gathered? Or the seven loaves for the four thousand, and how many baskets you gathered? How is it that you fail to understand that I did not speak about bread?"

MATTHEW 16:8–11

Lord, how often I am like the disciples! When I fixate on earthly concerns, I fail to grasp the wisdom You offer. When I focus only on the problems, I forget how You are able to take care of me in miraculous ways. Deepen my faith, Lord. Open my heart to Your truth. I pray for eyes and ears to understand so that I will never miss out on all You have to give. Amen.

THINK ABOUT IT:

Is a misplaced perspective preventing you from taking hold of something important?

No Fear

But he was in the stern, asleep on the cushion. And they woke him and said to him, "Teacher, do you not care that we are perishing?" And he awoke and rebuked the wind and said to the sea, "Peace! Be still!" And the wind ceased, and there was a great calm. He said to them, "Why are you so afraid? Have you still no faith?"

MARK 4:38-40

Lord, at first glance, Your words to Your disciples seem harsh. Tossed in a tiny boat on the sea, waves crashing overhead, no hope in sight. . . the situation looked dire. Because they weren't looking to You in faith. With You as Lord, what do I have to be afraid of? Pain—You will comfort me. Loneliness—You are with me. Need—You will provide. Uncertainty—You see ahead. Inability—You will see me through. Safety—You hold my life in Your hand. You are God. May I always have faith in You. Amen.

THINK ABOUT IT:

Why are you afraid?

Comfort: Pass It Along

*Blessed be the God and Father of our Lord Jesus Christ, the Father of
mercies and God of all comfort, who comforts us in all our affliction,
so that we may be able to comfort those who are in any affliction,
with the comfort with which we ourselves are comforted by God.*

2 CORINTHIANS 1:3-4

God, everyone needs someone to come beside them, to walk hand in
hand during difficult times. You have not left us alone to withstand the
battles; You come alongside us in hardship, offering strength and courage
to continue. When I would wilt under pressure, You uphold me. And
You call me to be a fellow comforter. Just as I experience the comfort of
knowing I am not alone, I will extend a hand to others and be a witness
to Your care. Amen.

THINK ABOUT IT:

Who needs God's comfort—via you—today?

Love in Service

Above all, keep loving one another earnestly, since love covers a multitude of sins. . . . As each has received a gift, use it to serve one another, as good stewards of God's varied grace: whoever speaks, as one who speaks oracles of God; whoever serves, as one who serves by the strength that God supplies—in order that in everything God may be glorified.

1 PETER 4:8, 10–11

God, love puts another before self. It's seeking someone else's good—even when I've been treated badly. After all, in the greatest display of love, You did not turn Your back on me when sin separated me from You; You reached out and poured Your love over me. Your love encourages me to love others with the same measure. You've equipped me for that purpose. May I use my gifts for Your glory. Amen.

THINK ABOUT IT:

What is it about God's love and grace that prompts
us to extend love and grace to others?

All in Good Time

For everything there is a season, and a time for every matter under heaven.... What gain has the worker from his toil? I have seen the business that God has given to the children of man to be busy with. He has made everything beautiful in its time.

ECCLESIASTES 3:1, 9–11

God, how much there is to do, how many things to accomplish! Remind me that just as You order nature, You appoint the seasons of my life—in Your perfect timing. Sometimes I rush ahead; sometimes I lag behind. But You, God, know exactly where I should be. Help me surrender my goals to You. Only when I'm in step with Your timing will I find satisfaction. I have confidence that You will make every season of my life beautiful in its time. Amen.

THINK ABOUT IT:

How can you find contentment in this season
of your life—whether ugly or beautiful?

Old and New

...to put off your old self, which belongs to your former manner of life and is corrupt through deceitful desires, and to be renewed in the spirit of your minds, and to put on the new self, created after the likeness of God in true righteousness and holiness.

EPHESIANS 4:22-24

Lord, You hear us say it—"Time for a change!" From our hairstyle, to our wardrobe, to the paint color on our walls, to our jobs, change can bring a new perspective, a feeling of beginning anew with fresh possibilities. The difference between old and new. When we come to You, Lord, You change us. We're able to shed the old self, which is full of sin, and don a new self. I need Your help in the process. Remove the hardened, dull layers until You reveal the gem underneath. Renew my mind with Your Word so I reflect from within Your holiness. Amen.

THINK ABOUT IT:

What does your new self look like in Christ?

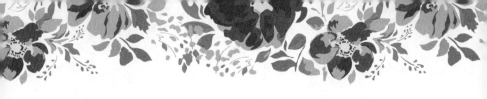

An All-You-Can-Forgive Mentality

Then Peter came up and said to him, "Lord, how often will my brother sin against me, and I forgive him? As many as seven times?" Jesus said to him, "I do not say to you seven times, but seventy-seven times."

MATTHEW 18:21-22

God, at times I struggle to forgive. When others hurt me—sometimes again and again—I am tempted to remain bitter and angry. I feel like they don't deserve forgiveness and often don't care if I offer it. It's easy to want to hold on to wrongs rather than release the burden. But then I think of Your forgiveness toward me. How many times have You granted forgiveness? More times than I care to count. Help me forgive as You forgive—lavishly. Generously. Lovingly. Through my forgiving heart, I reveal Your forgiving nature. Amen.

THINK ABOUT IT:

God's forgiveness is a gift to us—how is choosing to forgive a gift to yourself as well as to the one who wronged you?

The Devil, Withstood

*Your adversary the devil prowls around like a roaring lion,
seeking someone to devour. Resist him, firm in your faith,
knowing that the same kinds of suffering are being experienced
by your brotherhood throughout the world. And after you
have suffered a little while, the God of all grace, who has
called you to his eternal glory in Christ, will himself
restore, confirm, strengthen, and establish you.*

1 PETER 5:8-10

God, the devil is a master sidetracker. He would like nothing more than to push me off course through temptation and discouragement. He seeks to *devour*—strong word, for a serious threat. But Your Word says to resist, to stand strong in my faith. I will continue on the path You have set before me. I will not waver in obedience to You. Use this time, God, to deepen my faith and character. You will bring me through—better than before. Amen.

THINK ABOUT IT:

Does knowing that God Himself is perfecting
you encourage you to resist Satan?

Light to See

"Your eye is the lamp of your body. When your eye is healthy, your whole body is full of light, but when it is bad, your body is full of darkness. Therefore be careful lest the light in you be darkness. If then your whole body is full of light, having no part dark, it will be wholly bright, as when a lamp with its rays gives you light."

LUKE 11:34-36

Father, when my physical vision is murky, when I can't clearly see even my hand in front of my face, life will be hard. The same is true of spiritual sight. When I can't perceive Your truth, life will be difficult. I pray for clear spiritual vision, Father, for eyes to see Your truth. With healthy vision, my whole being is full of life-giving light. Amen.

THINK ABOUT IT:

How does faulty spiritual eyesight affect the whole of you—from your actions to your beliefs?

Counted

You have kept count of my tossings; put my tears in your bottle.
Are they not in your book?... This I know, that God is for me. In God,
whose word I praise, in the LORD, whose word I praise, in God I trust.

When I'm tossing and turning at night, Lord, it's easy to feel alone with grief or worries. The world is still—at rest—while my heart is restless. All is quiet except for my tears. But You are there. And not only do You witness my struggle, but You count my tossings; You collect my tears as they fall. It's not just another lost night of sleep. You take note of it. Lord, King David had much to fear when he wrote Psalm 56. Yet he knew one thing with certainty: You were for him. I place my trust, my praise, with You too, because You are for me. Amen.

THINK ABOUT IT:

Have you ever considered that your
restless nights are not lost on God?

Eat Your Fill

"Why do you spend your money for that which is not bread, and your labor for that which does not satisfy? Listen diligently to me, and eat what is good, and delight yourselves in rich food. Incline your ear, and come to me; hear, that your soul may live."

ISAIAH 55:2–3

Father, are You frustrated with all the ways I try to fill my soul apart from You, as I run around seeking comfort in buying things, in working to build a nest here on earth? When will I learn—for good—that nothing, absolutely nothing, will fill me like You? While earthly pursuits alone will leave me hungry for more, what You provide satisfies deeply. I turn to Your Word for the rich food—the joy, the peace, the assurance—that gives life. Amen.

THINK ABOUT IT:

Do you go to the world or God first to find satisfaction?

The Master's Plan

"Woe to him who strives with him who formed him, a pot among earthen pots! Does the clay say to him who forms it, 'What are you making?' or 'Your work has no handles'? Woe to him who says to a father, 'What are you begetting?' or to a woman, 'With what are you in labor?' "

ISAIAH 45:9–10

Father, like a child, at times I don't understand why certain things happen in my life. And I can't always see the purpose in Your plans for me. In my heart, I throw a tantrum and pout when my desires don't align with Your sovereign will. Quiet my soul, Father, long enough for me to hear You speak: "Be still. I am God." You only have my good in mind as You form my life. Please grant me patience as I wait for Your plans to unfold. I trust in Your design. Amen.

THINK ABOUT IT:

Is it difficult to rest in God's work when
the result isn't what you expected?

Quarrel-less

*Have nothing to do with foolish, ignorant controversies; you know
that they breed quarrels. And the Lord's servant must not be
quarrelsome—but kind to everyone, able to teach, patiently enduring
evil, correcting his opponents with gentleness. God may perhaps
grant them repentance leading to a knowledge of the truth.*

2 TIMOTHY 2:23–25

Quarrels. Bickering. God, as Your children, You would have us avoid
the ugliness of arguments. When we do speak out, we shouldn't mirror
the world that seeks to be "right" no matter what. We are to speak with
kindness. Gentleness. You are the master of using any situation for Your
good. You can use our words to draw others to You. Or if we are rude
and uncaring, we can repel others just as quickly. Act as a holy filter in
my mind, God, that only beauty would flow from me. Amen.

THINK ABOUT IT:

Is there a greater cost to ugly quarrels—
even if what you seek to point out is meant well?

If Not for Love

If I speak in the tongues of men and of angels, but have not love, I am a noisy gong or a clanging cymbal. And if I have prophetic powers, and understand all mysteries and all knowledge, and if I have all faith, so as to remove mountains, but have not love, I am nothing. If I give away all I have. . .but have not love, I gain nothing.

1 CORINTHIANS 13:1–3

Father, in Your Book, everything hinges on love. "For God so loved." Your great love put in motion Your plan of salvation, the greatest news the world has ever heard. The centrality of love should reflect in my life. I could do many remarkable deeds, but if they do not begin with love, they amount to nothing. I can do lots out of selfishness, but what really counts is what I do out of love. Fix my life on love, I pray. Amen.

THINK ABOUT IT:

How can love become a starting point for all you do?

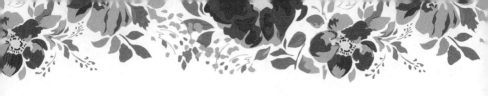

History of Doing

I will give thanks to the LORD with my whole heart; I will recount all of your wonderful deeds. I will be glad and exult in you; I will sing praise to your name, O Most High. . . . And those who know your name put their trust in you, for you, O LORD, have not forsaken those who seek you.

PSALM 9:1–2, 10

God, Your Word is a rich history of Your faithfulness and wonderful deeds. Across generations and through turbulent times, You have remained steadfast. A firm rock, an unwavering focus, a guarantee. You, God, I can count on! With each day, You are writing a rich history in my own life. From Your willingness to forgive—again—to the times You've stood by me, strengthening me in hardship and celebrating in joy, to Your rescuing hand when I've all but given up, You remain. I praise You, and I thank You, for all You've done. Amen.

THINK ABOUT IT:

What "wonderful deeds" has God done in Your life?

Like Hagar

And as she sat opposite him, she lifted up her voice and wept.
And God heard the voice of the boy, and the angel of God called
to Hagar from heaven and said to her, "What troubles you,
Hagar? Fear not, for God has heard the voice of the boy
where he is. Up! Lift up the boy, and hold him fast with
your hand, for I will make him into a great nation."

GENESIS 21:16–18

I can only imagine how Hagar felt, Lord. Used by Sarah to gain a child then cast aside; now wandering in the wilderness and in dread of her son's death. While it appeared that everyone had abandoned her and all was lost, You heard! You protected Hagar and Ishmael. You planned a future. Lord, in my most desperate times, remind me of Hagar. You follow us to the remotest places. You have a plan even when all seems hopeless. Amen.

THINK ABOUT IT:

How does Hagar's story encourage you?

You Are What You Bear

"For no good tree bears bad fruit, nor again does a bad tree bear good fruit, for each tree is known by its own fruit. For figs are not gathered from thornbushes, nor are grapes picked from a bramble bush. The good person out of the good treasure of his heart produces good, and the evil person out of his evil treasure produces evil."

LUKE 6:43–45

Lord, this is such a simple illustration but so true. Good trees bear good fruit. Likewise, out of a good heart, good flows. I can't harbor sin and ugliness and expect to yield good in my life. But if I fill myself with good—Your Word, Your love, Your will—good is the result. Help me clear out the brambles, Lord, and replace them with healthy fruit. I want others to recognize You when they see the good in me. May I be known for good! Amen.

THINK ABOUT IT:

What do you consider good fruit in the life of a Christian?

My Manna

Then the LORD said to Moses, "Behold, I am about to rain bread
from heaven for you, and the people shall go out and gather
a day's portion every day, that I may test them,
whether they will walk in my law or not."

EXODUS 16:4

God, as I read about the Israelites in the wilderness, I sometimes catch myself being critical. You told them how and when to collect manna; You revealed Your plan clearly. Yet some doubted; they disobeyed. How foolish! God, You tell me in Your Word that You will take care of me. You teach me to be content, to trust, to pray: "Give us day by day our daily bread" (Luke 11:3 KJV). Yet at times I doubt You and carve my own way through the wilderness. How foolish! I choose today to rest in Your sovereign plan. Amen.

THINK ABOUT IT:

How are you like the Israelites when faced
with the test of trusting in God's provision?

Steady as a Rock

*"Everyone who comes to me and hears my words and does them,
I will show you what he is like: he is like a man building a house,
who dug deep and laid the foundation on the rock. And when
a flood arose, the stream broke against that house and
could not shake it, because it had been well built."*

LUKE 6:47-48

Lord, You were a teacher to Your disciples. What You told them was for their good, their best. The same is true for me. Through Your Word You lead me and teach me, and what I hear, even if I don't understand, is for my good, my best. I can choose to build my life on Your commands and have a firm base when stormy times come, or I can live without Your foundation and fall apart. I choose to listen and do Your will. Amen.

THINK ABOUT IT:

How is God's Word like a rock for your life?

Ill Fitted

*But Moses said to the L*ORD, *"Oh, my Lord, I am not eloquent, either in the past or since you have spoken to your servant. . . ." Then the L*ORD *said to him, "Who has made man's mouth? Who makes him mute, or deaf, or seeing, or blind? Is it not I, the L*ORD*? Now therefore go, and I will be with your mouth and teach you what you shall speak."*

EXODUS 4:10-12

Father, in service, in relationships, in missions, in parenting, in jobs—in the many roles we are called to fill—how often do we feel like Moses? Ill equipped, ill at ease, ill suited. . .we don't measure up! When I feel like this, Father, remind me that You made me just as I am. Your plan for my life is custom fit—even my weaknesses. You will be there upholding me in the roles You call me to. Be with me as I go, I pray. Amen.

THINK ABOUT IT:

Is God using limitations to strengthen your faith?

Spirit of the Sabbath

And he said to them, "The Sabbath was made for man, not man for the Sabbath. So the Son of Man is lord even of the Sabbath."

MARK 2:27-28

A day of rest! Lord, with all the responsibilities of living, it's easy to become tired or even exhausted. As to-do lists lengthen, time to rejuvenate seems to shorten day by day until resting is all but forgotten. You have designed me wonderfully, and part of that design is rest. A time to put aside work and trust in Your provision. A time to abandon worldly pursuits and turn my heart heavenward in worship. A time to reset for the week ahead. Lord, Your Sabbath is a beautiful reflection of how You created, resting on the seventh day, and how You continue to care for Your creation. May I never forget Your blessing or twist it into duty but keep it as You intended: a day of rest. Amen.

THINK ABOUT IT:

How can you establish a Sabbath rest this week?

Like Water

*"For as the rain and the snow come down from heaven and do not
return there but water the earth, making it bring forth and sprout,
giving seed to the sower and bread to the eater, so shall my word
be that goes out from my mouth; it shall not return to me
empty, but it shall accomplish that which I purpose,
and shall succeed in the thing for which I sent it."*

ISAIAH 55:10–11

Father, water is so essential to life. Every living thing needs it—from plants to humans. It rains down from the sky to support life, and it does. I can see how water falling on parched ground brings renewal; water causes delicate saplings to grow. Your Word is like the water. With it we quench our thirsty souls and nourish our faith. And just as physical water meets physical needs, Your Word will not fail to meet our spiritual needs. Thank You for sending Your Word. Amen.

THINK ABOUT IT:

What spiritual needs does God's Word fulfill?

Burden Bearers

If anyone is caught in any transgression, you who are spiritual should restore him in a spirit of gentleness. Keep watch on yourself, lest you too be tempted. Bear one another's burdens, and so fulfill the law of Christ.

GALATIANS 6:1–2

Lord, we all struggle with walking in Christlike ways at times. We all have weaknesses and fail in the face of temptation. Bearing the burden alone can be overwhelming, and we would fall under its weight. Thank You for those You place in our lives who come alongside to shoulder the burdens together. May I be that person for someone. May I be a source of encouragement, accountability, strength, and prayer. As I reach out in love and faith, guard my heart, Lord. Keep me steady to help support another, I pray. Amen.

THINK ABOUT IT:

How have your sisters in Christ been a
blessing when you struggle with sin?

Heaven Awaits

"Now God's presence is with people, and he will live with them, and they will be his people. God himself will be with them and will be their God. He will wipe away every tear from their eyes, and there will be no more death, sadness, crying, or pain, because all the old ways are gone." The One who was sitting on the throne said, "Look! I am making everything new!"

REVELATION 21:3-5 NCV

God, heaven sounds like. . .heaven! I can only begin to imagine all that it will be. A place with no more tears, no more death, no more pain. This old life that is so wearisome will be gone, replaced with new, perfect life. Even more unimaginable: You will dwell with us. What we have only begun to experience through Your Holy Spirit in our hearts will surround us. What a glorious place it will be! Thank You for the promise of heaven, God. Amen.

THINK ABOUT IT:

What do you look forward to most in heaven?

Wonderfully Made

For you formed my inward parts; you knitted me together in my mother's womb. I praise you, for I am fearfully and wonderfully made.... Your eyes saw my unformed substance; in your book were written, every one of them, the days that were formed for me, when as yet there was none of them.

PSALM 139:13-14, 16

Father, when I look in the mirror, sometimes I begin to pick apart what You lovingly created. Why not a different nose? Different hair, skin? Why not a thinner this, curvier that? In these moments, Father, remind me of the words of the psalm. You formed every cell of me before I was born. My body is miraculous in all its uniqueness. And more than just creating the physical me, You form my days before I live them. You are master of body and life. I praise You for Your design. Amen.

THINK ABOUT IT:

Do you look at yourself and your life with criticism or praise?

She Laughed. . .

So Sarah laughed to herself, saying, "After I am worn out, and my lord is old, shall I have pleasure?" The LORD said to Abraham, "Why did Sarah laugh and say, 'Shall I indeed bear a child, now that I am old?' Is anything too hard for the LORD?"

GENESIS 18:12–14

God, You are almighty. You reign over heaven and earth. Considering that, Sarah's laughter itself is laughable. How could she laugh at Your promise, Your plan? But we all are Sarahs at times, aren't we? Whether we doubt Your ability or dislike the timing, we lack faith. God, forgive me for my Sarah moments. Open my faith wide so that I view my life with You in mind. Nothing is too hard for You. Through the seemingly impossible ways You work, Your glory shines. Amen.

THINK ABOUT IT:

How does God use Sarah's example and our own "Sarah moments" to teach us about Himself?

Child of God

The disciples came to Jesus, saying, "Who is the greatest in the
kingdom of heaven?" And calling to him a child, he put him in the
midst of them and said, "Truly, I say to you, unless you turn
and become like children, you will never enter the kingdom
of heaven. Whoever humbles himself like this child
is the greatest in the kingdom of heaven."

MATTHEW 18:1-4

The greatest in Your kingdom, Lord, will have childlike faith. The disciples were focused on what they could achieve to be the greatest, but You showed them that it is what they believe that makes them great in Your sight. To approach You as a child means trusting You as my heavenly Father. To approach You as a child means resting in Your care. To approach You as a child means looking to You for all my needs. I sit at Your feet today as Your child. Amen.

THINK ABOUT IT:

What are some examples of God taking
the least and making it great?

Inner Adornment

Do not let your adorning be external—the braiding of hair and
the putting on of gold jewelry, or the clothing you wear—but let
your adorning be the hidden person of the heart with the
imperishable beauty of a gentle and quiet spirit,
which in God's sight is very precious.

1 PETER 3:3-4

God, what's on the outside is important to most women. From our hair to our shoes and everything in between, we expend a lot of time, energy, money, and thought on how to adorn our physical selves. While You bless us with beautiful things, real beauty—a beauty that will outlast even the most precious jewels—resides in our hearts. A beautiful spirit is precious to You, God. Each day, may I pour more effort into beautifying my spirit than my body. May I be truly gorgeous in Your sight. Amen.

THINK ABOUT IT:

Why is a gentle and quiet spirit beautiful?

Of Heaven

*"These things I speak in the world, that they may have my joy fulfilled
in themselves. I have given them your word, and the world has hated
them because they are not of the world, just as I am not of the
world. I do not ask that you take them out of the world,
but that you keep them from the evil one."*

JOHN 17:13–15

A square among polka dots. Lord, as a Christian it's natural to feel out
of place in the world. Once I believed in You, my true home became a
future home in heaven. And while I *feel* at odds, the world should *see*
me as different. A daughter of the King with a mission to spread Your
love—even if it is met with hate. Lord, You knew that Your disciples, You
knew that I, would experience this. So You prayed. You prayed for our
protection. You prayed for our joy. Thank You for Your prayers. Amen.

THINK ABOUT IT:

What is Christ's prayer for you?

Small but Mighty

No one can tame the tongue. It is wild and evil and full of deadly poison. We use our tongues to praise our Lord and Father, but then we curse people, whom God made like himself. Praises and curses come from the same mouth! My brothers and sisters, this should not happen.

JAMES 3:8-10 NCV

Sticks and stones can break my bones. . .and words can wound even deeper. God, the tongue, and the words it forms, has great power. Power for good as I bless and pray and praise, but also power to curse and do harm. When ugly words slip out, the truth of James is so clear. Who can tame the tongue? Only You. Use my tongue to speak of Your love, Your healing, with words that penetrate to the soul and uplift. May my words always be in harmony with my faith. Amen.

THINK ABOUT IT:

Do you need to ask God for a tongue taming?

E-V-E-R-Y

Rejoice always, pray without ceasing, give thanks in all circumstances; for this is the will of God in Christ Jesus for you.

1 THESSALONIANS 5:16–18

When I read these words in 1 Thessalonians, God, they seem so simple, and yet doing them seems impossible. Rejoice *always*. Pray *without ceasing*. Give thanks *in all circumstances*. How can that be? How can I keep up? Because of You. Because of Your love and salvation, every moment is cause for joy. Because of Your promise to hear me when I cry out in faith, every need, every answer, is a reason to never give up on prayer. Because of Your presence, every day I can give thanks no matter what happens. I won't be perfect, but place in me a heart to rejoice, to pray, to offer thanks continually. Amen.

THINK ABOUT IT:

What ways can joy, prayer, and gratitude
become essential parts of everyday life?

Higher Thoughts

If then you have been raised with Christ, seek the things that are above, where Christ is, seated at the right hand of God. Set your minds on things that are above, not on things that are on earth. For you have died, and your life is hidden with Christ in God. When Christ who is your life appears, then you also will appear with him in glory.

COLOSSIANS 3:1–4

When You redeem my life at the moment of salvation, Lord, You reserve a place for me in heaven. My new life is hidden with You above, yet my mind lags behind as my thoughts still center on this life. It's easy to get discouraged when my focus is downward instead of heavenward. It's easy to become distracted when my eyes aren't on You. Lord, set my mind on things above. May I never lose sight of my new life and my future home. Amen.

THINK ABOUT IT:

Do this life's disappointments pale when
seen in the light of heaven's hope?

Bold Spirit

*For this reason I remind you to fan into flame the gift of
God, which is in you through the laying on of my hands,
for God gave us a spirit not of fear but of power and love.*

2 TIMOTHY 1:6-7

God, You want me to be bold. When I use the gift You have given me and walk in Your will, You equip me, not with fear, but with power, with love. Far from a shriveling flower, cowering in the shade, I can bloom. I can stand tall, knowing that You have supplied all I need to weather even the harshest times. I can bring brightness by living out and sharing Your love. Just as Paul told Timothy to fan into flame his gift, remind me each morning to cultivate my gift. May it flourish in power and love. Amen.

THINK ABOUT IT:

How can you bring a renewed energy to using your spiritual gift?

A Clean Sweep

Create in me a clean heart, O God, and renew a right spirit within me. Cast me not away from your presence, and take not your Holy Spirit from me. Restore to me the joy of your salvation, and uphold me with a willing spirit.

PSALM 51:10–12

God, I know how good it feels to spring-clean, to reorganize and refresh my home. Getting rid of ignored cobwebs and dust, letting a fresh breeze flow in, removing clutter, and opening up space... Much more important is the "spring-cleaning" You can do in me. Sweep out sin to reveal a clean heart, God. Breathe into my life so I approach today and the days to come with a renewed spirit. Open me to Your joy, I pray. It feels so good to start fresh! Amen.

THINK ABOUT IT:

What areas of your life need a little spring-cleaning?

The Shelter of His Wings

*He will cover you with his feathers, and under his wings
you can hide. His truth will be your shield and protection.*

PSALM 91:4 NCV

Father, in Your design You have programmed in us the comfort of a hug. When a child falls and scrapes her knee or awakes at night from a bad dream, a hug can soothe and let her know that she is not alone. A hug means belonging, being wrapped in love. Even the birds of Your creation know the power of gathering precious ones together. As a parent bird enfolds and guides and protects chicks with loving wings, so You, our heavenly Father, enfold Your children, guiding and protecting us with Your love. Cover me today; let me hide in Your care. Amen.

THINK ABOUT IT:

Have there been moments in your life when you felt
God's love surround you like wings of refuge?

More Than Lip Service

Let the words of my mouth and the meditation of my heart be
acceptable in your sight, O Lord, my rock and my redeemer.

PSALM 19:14

In Old Testament times, God, those who worshipped You made sacrifices—physical displays of their devotion. They prayed that the sacrifices would be acceptable. Today, Christians are living sacrifices; it is with our lives that we show worship and devotion. God, I pray along with King David that my "sacrifices" go deep—beyond physical. I want the meditation of my heart—what my heart dwells on—to be pleasing to You. Then from a heart attitude of sacrifice will flow words of beauty, reflections of the God my life is sacrificed for. May my words and heart be acceptable in Your sight. Amen.

THINK ABOUT IT:

Do you believe God cares just as much about your
inner self as He does what others hear or see?

The First Step

If we confess our sins, he is faithful and just to forgive us our sins and to cleanse us from all unrighteousness.

1 JOHN 1:9

God, thank You for forgiveness. Because of Your awesome love, You chose not to stand aside and let me perish in my sin but provided a way out, a way to You. Without You, God, I have no future, but with You I have life. Because of Your precious Son's death and resurrection, I chose Your saving grace. Now as Your child, when sin confronts me, I must take the first step. I must confess my sin. . .then in Your faithfulness, You will forgive. Incredible! May I never take Your forgiveness for granted but always reach for Your help after I stumble. You will wipe the dirt from my knees and set me on the path again. Amen.

THINK ABOUT IT:

Do you sometimes skip confession in prayer, assuming that God has forgiven by default?

Where Are You Going?

Let me hear in the morning of your steadfast love, for in you I trust.
Make me know the way I should go, for to you I lift up my soul.

PSALM 143:8

Father, direction is important in life. North, south, east, west...knowing where I'm headed keeps me focused, keeps me in line with Your will. But I'm only human. My compass is faulty. It points to my desires and comfort and ease as true north, even when the best way might be the opposite way. I need Your compass, Father. Each morning as I face a new day, grant me a keen desire to bend my knees and ask for Your direction. You love me, steadfastly. I can trust You, completely. Point me in the right direction, I pray. Amen.

THINK ABOUT IT:

Have you ever felt as if God's leading is off—
but later discovered that He had you right on course?

Wise Words

But the wisdom from above is first pure, then peaceable, gentle,
open to reason, full of mercy and good fruits, impartial and sincere.

JAMES 3:17

Father, if women are supposedly born communicators, why do we struggle with the ugly side of communicating? Gossip, quarrels, backbiting. . .we use our words to hurt rather than heal, to uplift ourselves instead of uplifting others. We want to be heard first and listen later; we try to be polished when we should be honest. There's still so much we can learn about communicating! We can become so much *wiser* with our words. Teach us how, Father. Describing wisdom, James used the words *pure, peaceable, gentle, reason, mercy, good, impartial, sincere.* The beautiful side of communicating. May I think on these words before I speak. May I become a wise communicator, I pray. Amen.

THINK ABOUT IT:

How can you incorporate James' words
on wisdom into your relationships?

A Hand to Hold

*For I, the LORD your God, hold your right hand; it is I who
say to you, "Fear not, I am the one who helps you."*

ISAIAH 41:13

God, when I think about holding hands, I envision beautiful things. I
see a father reaching out to grasp his child's hand before they cross a
busy street. I see two people in love walking side by side. I see hands
held to comfort and reassure in times of trial. I see hands held in unity
when facing opposition—and raised together in triumph. But more
beautiful than all these is the thought of You holding my hand as You
guide my steps. As You pour out Your love and encouragement. As You
uphold me; as You celebrate with me. You, my God, stand beside me,
hand clasped. Amen.

THINK ABOUT IT:

What has God's presence meant to you
in troubling and joyous times?

No Standard-Issue Peace

"Peace I leave with you; my peace I give to you. Not as the world gives do I give to you. Let not your hearts be troubled, neither let them be afraid."

JOHN 14:27

Lord, I've heard it said, "Pray for peace." I pray for peace—that there be an ease in conflict and that hurting souls find relief. But I also pray for *Your* peace in my life. Your peace goes deep. Your peace is a sense of calm that let You sleep even during a raging storm at sea. Your peace offered security in Your Father's will—even when following led to anguish and a cross. Your peace means hope in hopeless situations, comfort during pain, a future when all seems lost. This kind of peace comes only from You, Lord. I need a dose today; please settle me with Your deep peace. Amen.

THINK ABOUT IT:

How is Christ's peace different from the world's?

Show. . .

Was not also Rahab the prostitute justified by works when she received the messengers and sent them out by another way? For as the body apart from the spirit is dead, so also faith apart from works is dead.

JAMES 2:25-26

Father, from the outside and at first glance, Rahab doesn't seem like a faith-filled woman. Her occupation is less than holy and she lies to help the messengers, but deep inside her faith is true. Putting herself in great risk, she takes a stand for You. She remains a reflection of faith lived out, a reflection of each godly woman. Father, sin is a part of all of us; and while You abhor sin, You extend grace to sinners. I pray that my faith shines brighter than my sin so those who see my life will know that I'm alive in You. Amen.

THINK ABOUT IT:

What ways can you show that your faith is a living faith?

...And Tell

Jesus said to her, "I who speak to you am he." ... So the woman left her water jar and went away into town and said to the people, "Come, see a man who told me all that I ever did. Can this be the Christ?"

JOHN 4:26, 28-29

Lord, I confess the Samaritan woman's response humbles and challenges me. Because of her reputation, she was an outcast among outcasts to the Jewish people. Yet once You reached out to her and she embraced You, she was bold to tell her story, to tell Your story. She did not tuck what she'd received deep inside but abandoned her water jug and went straightaway to share with others. Too often I shrink from telling how You continually transform my life. Forgive me, Lord. Embolden me! Let nothing—my past or what's to come—keep me silent. Amen.

THINK ABOUT IT:

How are you like the Samaritan woman?
How can you become more like her?

Remember When

And he said to the people of Israel, "When your children ask their fathers in times to come, 'What do these stones mean?' then you shall let your children know, 'Israel passed over this Jordan on dry ground.' For the LORD your God dried up the waters of the Jordan for you until you passed over."

JOSHUA 4:21-23

God, the Bible is a rich record of what You've done in the lives of believers. Remembering Your mighty works keeps us praising You and following You, even in grim moments. Besides reading the biblical accounts, God, remind us that we, as families and as a community, have our own rich history to pass down to the children in our lives. Please show us ways to mark the times You have come through for us. There are so many! Use our memories to fill the next generation with Your truth so that they never forget. Amen.

THINK ABOUT IT:

What events or periods of your life will you preserve?

Humble Me

[Christ Jesus], though he was in the form of God, did not count equality with God a thing to be grasped, but emptied himself, by taking the form of a servant, being born in the likeness of men. And being found in human form, he humbled himself by becoming obedient to the point of death, even death on a cross.

PHILIPPIANS 2:6–8

Lord, You embody humility—something that seems foreign in our culture. Everywhere, I see people who prize being "better than," who look after themselves before others. I'm guilty of the same mind-set more than I'd like to admit, Lord. It's not easy to put *self* aside. In part, that's what makes You remarkable, Your love incomprehensible. You are one with God, yet You "emptied" Yourself, humbled Yourself, in order for me to thrive. Remind me of Your great humility as I approach my days emptied of self and ready to serve. Amen.

THINK ABOUT IT:

Why is being truly humble so hard?

Clear the Air

"So when you offer your gift to God at the altar, and you remember that your brother or sister has something against you, leave your gift there at the altar. Go and make peace with that person, and then come and offer your gift."

MATTHEW 5:23-24 NCV

Grudges, tiffs, squabbles...whatever we call them, and however justified they are, Father, they get in the way of true worship. You sacrificed everything to reconcile us to You, to heal a severed relationship. Why should we not do everything in our power to right what is wrong before praising You? Prod my heart, Father. Don't let me ignore conflict out of pride or a false sense of entitlement. You know what's best for me when I'm blinded by emotion. "Go...make peace," Jesus said. May I do just that. Amen.

THINK ABOUT IT:

Do you need to make peace with someone today?

Home Away from Home

"In my Father's house are many rooms. If it were not so, would I have told you that I go to prepare a place for you? And if I go and prepare a place for you, I will come again and will take you to myself, that where I am you may be also."

JOHN 14:2-3

Home. Lord, that word can mean so many good things. A place of belonging, a safe haven. . .it's where the heart is. But this world can rip "home" from us. Dysfunctional families, foreclosures, natural disasters, rising rent—sadly, our home on earth isn't always so good. While we can't count on the blessing of a sound earthly home, we can count on Your promise of a glorious home to come. There we will have a place beyond anything we imagine. There we will be home. Amen.

THINK ABOUT IT:

What do you look forward to most in your heavenly homecoming?

This Little Light

If you feed those who are hungry and take care of the needs of those who are troubled, then your light will shine in the darkness, and you will be bright like sunshine at noon.

Isaiah 58:10 NCV

God, I want to shine! This world is so dark; there are so many needs. From my own backyard to places I've never been far across the world, people are hungry for relief and hungry for Your love. My soul aches at the pain, but sometimes I feel helpless to help. But I'm not, God—not with You to lead me. Expose my discouragement for what it is: one of the devil's lies. Show me ways I can brighten dark corners with the blessings You've poured out to me. Be with me as I shine, God. Amen.

THINK ABOUT IT:

How can you shine—even a glimmer—into others' lives this week? This month? This year?

Bread of Life

Jesus then said to them, "Truly, truly, I say to you, it was not Moses who gave you the bread from heaven, but my Father gives you the true bread from heaven. For the bread of God is he who comes down from heaven and gives life to the world."

JOHN 6:32-33

Thank You, Lord, for true bread. When speaking about the nourishment You provide, You first reminded the disciples of the miracle manna. For forty years manna sustained physical life as the Israelites traveled in the wilderness. But with Your arrival on earth dawned an even greater power—God's power to sustain eternal life. Ordinary bread, even supernatural manna, only meets temporary needs, but You, Lord, fill souls to the brim. Never will I be truly hungry with You, the "bread of life" (John 6:35). Amen.

THINK ABOUT IT:

Do you say grace before meals? How can you begin to thank God daily for the spiritual nourishment He bestows?

For Good, for God

"Be especially careful when you are trying to be good so that you don't make a performance out of it. It might be good theater, but the God who made you won't be applauding."

MATTHEW 6:1 MSG

Father, applause is sweet to our ears. We long to hear an *atta girl* in response to what we do. While encouragement has its place, my motivation for doing good begins and ends with You, Father. My offerings are still beautiful in Your sight if only You see them. My victory over temptation is still a cause for celebration if only the angels in heaven cheer me on. My acts of kindness, my whispered prayers, and my witness are just as powerful without applause. Keep me focused on You, my audience of One, when I act in goodness. Your applause is the sweetest of all. Amen.

THINK ABOUT IT:

Whose eyes are you most conscious of when you do good things?

Flesh and God

"And I will give you a new heart, and a new spirit I will put within you. And I will remove the heart of stone from your flesh and give you a heart of flesh."

EZEKIEL 36:26

God, I am amazed by the intricacy of Your creation, like the flesh that covers and protects me. Flesh can change. And just like cuts that mend, scars that fade, and muscles that strengthen, with a spiritual heart of flesh, You can heal me, renew me, grow me. You enter my life, and my heart changes. Once resistant, I now yield. Once unbendable, I'm now open to Your will. Once tough, I now respond to Your gentle prompting. Day by day, God, please continue to work within so that the very heart of me reflects You. Amen.

THINK ABOUT IT:

Why is a fleshy heart so important in the life of a Christian?

Not-So-Best Foot Forward

Many of the believers began to confess openly and tell all the
evil things they had done.... So in a powerful way the
word of the Lord kept spreading and growing.

ACTS 19:18, 20 NCV

Lord, sometimes it seems as if I'm surrounded by facades. You know what I mean—everyone trying to present their best self. Jaw-dropping multitasker, breezy artiste, business genius, wonder woman...whatever we show others, it's rarely our bad side. But You do Your greatest work in messy, imperfect lives. Why do we try to hide the not-quite-put-together side of us? Our flaws, our mistakes, our fears, our sins... You can use them to shout of Your grace. Grant me courage to share my *real* self—good side and bad—so that others hear of You through me. Amen.

THINK ABOUT IT:

When you think back on testimonies you've heard,
which ones were the most powerful?

The Power of Prayer

And when they had prayed, the place in which they were gathered together was shaken, and they were all filled with the Holy Spirit and continued to speak the word of God with boldness.

ACTS 4:31

Father, lately life has been so busy, and I've drifted from prayer. I send up a quick "Hi, goodbye" and then wonder why I don't feel You working in me. I kneel before You today asking for forgiveness. You deserve my best, not my leftovers. And amazingly, humblingly—You, almighty God, long for me, little me, to commune with You. Remind me of the privilege of prayer. Remind me of the *power* of prayer. Your disciples prayed and walls shook. Your children pray and Your Holy Spirit moves in us. Father, may prayer be a vital force in me, my lifeblood. Amen.

THINK ABOUT IT:

When have you seen prayer yield powerful results?

If Trees Could Talk

"But ask the animals, and they will teach you, or ask the birds of the air, and they will tell you. Speak to the earth, and it will teach you, or let the fish of the sea tell you.... The life of every creature and the breath of all people are in God's hand."

JOB 12:7–8, 10 NCV

God, the first place I go to learn about You is Your holy Word. There You have laid out a glorious résumé of who You are. But You've also written Yourself into nature. Lift my eyes to see Your creation, God. Beasts and birds and earth and sea helped Job grasp You in troubling times. By pausing to reflect on what's around me, I too can glimpse You. Your power to renew after ruin, Your splendor, Your provision, Your design for life . . . You are everywhere, in everything. Praise to You, God of all. Amen.

THINK ABOUT IT:

How can you spend some time experiencing God through nature?

No In-Between

" 'I know your works: you are neither cold nor hot. Would that you were either cold or hot! So, because you are lukewarm, and neither hot nor cold, I will spit you out of my mouth.' "
REVELATION 3:15-16

Lord, I don't like drinking stale, lukewarm water. It's neither comforting like something hot nor refreshing like something cold. These verses in Revelation say that You don't like lukewarm Christianity. It's somewhere between turning a cold shoulder and being on fire for God—and its superficiality sickens You. I want to be a Christian through and through, not declaring You as Lord and then living in the lukewarm. I want to be a hot Christian! Fill me, fuel me so that my every deed reveals a fervor for You. Amen.

THINK ABOUT IT:

If you are lukewarm in faith, what actions—like immersing yourself in the Bible and prayer—can heat up your Christianity?

Reciprocal

[Hannah] was deeply distressed and prayed to the LORD and wept bitterly. And she vowed a vow and said, "O LORD of hosts, if you will indeed look on the affliction of your servant and remember me and not forget your servant, but will give to your servant a son, then I will give him to the LORD all the days of his life."

1 SAMUEL 1:10–11

Lord, when I pray for something that I want deep down, it usually doesn't cross my mind to offer it right back up to You. But that's exactly what Hannah did. She desperately wanted a son. She wept and prayed for Your favor—and then she promised to return to You what You gave. Such a beautiful picture of faith beginning and ending with You. To receive and let go with open hands. . .to pray in gratitude and for Your glory. Lord, may what I want for *me* be ever focused on You. Amen.

THINK ABOUT IT:

Do you consider God in your prayer requests?

Take a Stand!

Then the king of Egypt said to the Hebrew midwives, one of whom was named Shiphrah and the other Puah, "When you serve as midwife to the Hebrew women and see them on the birthstool, if it is a son, you shall kill him...." But the midwives feared God and did not do as the king of Egypt commanded them.

EXODUS 1:15-17

God, Shiphrah and Puah were two gutsy women. Do I have the courage to do the crazy thing—the thing that puts me at risk to honor You? While I may never face such an extreme choice as these midwives, my life is made up of countless chances to choose You over the world. Be with me as You surely were with Shiphrah and Puah. Grant me the courage—in the everyday choices and even once-in-a-lifetime ones—not to cower or water down my faith, but instead remain true to You. Amen.

THINK ABOUT IT:

Why do we often fear humankind more than God?

Our Father in Heaven

The Spirit we received does not make us slaves again to fear; it makes us children of God. With that Spirit we cry out, "Father." And the Spirit himself joins with our spirits to say we are God's children.

ROMANS 8:15-16 NCV

Father! Abba! As I bow before You, God Almighty, remind me that You are also Daddy. In a miracle beyond understanding, I became Your daughter, and I now draw close and sit at Your feet without fear. I come to You for guidance. I come to You for comfort. I come to You in honesty, because You know the depths of me—my ugly and pretty—and love me just the same. Linger here awhile, Father, just the two of us, until I know what it means to hear You whisper, "My child." Amen.

THINK ABOUT IT:

Do you struggle to see God as your heavenly Father?
What makes you feel near to Him?

One, a Lonely Number

Two are better than one, because they have a good reward for their toil. For if they fall, one will lift up his fellow. But woe to him who is alone when he falls and has not another to lift him up!

ECCLESIASTES 4:9-10

God, You designed us for companionship. Adam worked the garden, but You knew he needed someone by his side to share the toil. Enter Eve. Your design has not changed with passing time. We still need others walking with us, working alongside us. Out of pride or fear of being a burden, how often do I fail to ask for help, to seek someone to share the load? I'm not perfect; I know that very well! Please place companions in my life to offer a hand up when I'm down—and place me in the path of others so I can do the same. Amen.

THINK ABOUT IT:

How have you seen the truth of these verses lived out in your life?

Forgiven

He does not deal with us according to our sins, nor repay us according to our iniquities. For as high as the heavens are above the earth, so great is his steadfast love toward those who fear him; as far as the east is from the west, so far does he remove our transgressions from us.

PSALM 103:10–12

Lord, how I needed the beauty of these words today! How I needed to remember their rich meaning. You don't love a little, forgive a little; You love and forgive vastly—as high as heaven above earth and as far as east from west. So often I receive Your forgiveness, but the sin taunts me, remaining just in sight, and I wonder that You could ever love me. Expose this for the lie it is. You remove my sin beyond sight; You love beyond understanding. All I can say is thank You! Amen.

THINK ABOUT IT:

Do you limit God's forgiveness? How can you embrace
the truth of the psalm—that His forgiveness is complete?

To Have a Friend. . .

Laugh with your happy friends when they're happy; share tears when they're down. Get along with each other; don't be stuck-up. Make friends with nobodies; don't be the great somebody.

ROMANS 12:15-16 MSG

Why does friendship sometimes seem so complicated, Lord? Friendships should be sources of support and joy, but so often conflict and hurt lace them. Instead of resting in their blessing, we labor under their weight. Lord, I read the words in Romans and begin to think that the problem starts in me—in each of us as individuals. Am I approaching friendship with the wrong focus? If my wish is first to *be* a friend and not just *receive* friendship, then my relationships have a chance to blossom. As I spend time with friends this week, refocus me on them, Lord. Amen.

THINK ABOUT IT:

How would your friendships change if you spent more time just being present for your friends?

Never Forsaken

*And about the ninth hour Jesus cried out with a loud voice,
saying, "Eli, Eli, lema sabachthani?" that is, "My God,
my God, why have you forsaken me?"*

MATTHEW 27:46

Lord, too often I think of the cross as just physical. You took my place and suffered brutality as I should have suffered for my sin. But more than the nail-pierced hands and agonizing death, You experienced God forsaking You. You endured unimaginable sorrow—out of boundless love. Because of You, I will never know the cost of sin, I will never feel God turn His back on me. . . Saying thank You will never be enough, Lord. So in humility I offer my life to You. When I am tempted to turn my back and follow my will instead of Yours, remind me of the cost I'll never pay. Obedience is such a small price in comparison! Amen.

THINK ABOUT IT:

What motivates you to remain faithful to God?

24-Karat Faith

These troubles come to prove that your faith is pure. This purity of faith is worth more than gold, which can be proved to be pure by fire but will ruin. But the purity of your faith will bring you praise and glory and honor when Jesus Christ is shown to you.

1 PETER 1:7 NCV

Father, I am in the middle of troubles, and it's hard to think clearly. It's hard to trust that I will benefit from something that seems to rip me apart. But I've been through rough waters before. Looking back, I can see where I have grown, where my faith has deepened. I know I will come through these difficult times too, with faith more precious and lasting than gold. I know that my full reward is yet to come. For now, may I thrive in assurance of faith, even in the middle of troubles. Amen.

THINK ABOUT IT:

How have trials made you more certain than ever of your faith?

Pesky, Purposeful Thorn

A thorn was given me in the flesh, a messenger of Satan to harass me,
to keep me from becoming conceited. Three times I pleaded with the
Lord about this, that it should leave me. But he said to me, "My grace
is sufficient for you, for my power is made perfect in weakness."

2 CORINTHIANS 12:7–9

Lord, I think I can empathize with Paul. There is something in my life that makes life difficult. I cry out to You to remove it over…and over…but You have a greater goal in mind. There is purpose in this circumstance. Help me see the *why*. What am I to learn? Please never let me forget that while You allow the hardship to remain, You don't abandon me to tough it out on my own. Your grace is always present. Your grace is always enough. Let Your glory shine through me, Lord. Amen.

THINK ABOUT IT:

What might be the purpose of a difficult
situation in your life right now?

Sorrow Not

But I would not have you to be ignorant, brethren, concerning them which are asleep, that ye sorrow not, even as others which have no hope. For if we believe that Jesus died and rose again, even so them also which sleep in Jesus will God bring with him.

1 THESSALONIANS 4:13–14 KJV

Father, words seem empty to describe what the death of a loved one means. Someone once close to us is now gone. But while we mourn for our loss, pour into us the truth of the words of these verses: we have hope in You! Tears may fall, but they will mingle with the promise of eternal life. Our ache, though deep, is only temporary, because in heaven our loved one will once again be near, forever. No more tears, just joy everlasting. We await that day, Father, with hope, not sadness. Amen.

THINK ABOUT IT:

What does it look like to grieve with hope?

Whatever You Do

So, whether you eat or drink, or whatever you do, do all to the glory of God. Give no offense to Jews or to Greeks or to the church of God, just as I try to please everyone in everything I do, not seeking my own advantage, but that of many, that they may be saved.

Lord, it feels as if I've grown up in a culture that's all about personal liberty—"what suits me" instead of "what benefits you." Humans can be very self-centered—myself included. But You would flip this mind-set on its head. From the moment You were born, Your agenda was others-centered. I'll admit, it's not easy, Lord. I need You for me to succeed. Keep me centered outward. Help me see the little things that seem *so* important for what they are—mere specks in the light of Your great salvation. Amen.

THINK ABOUT IT:

How often do you consider others—
and God—in the personal choices you make?

Prayer 101

Now Jesus was praying in a certain place, and when he finished, one of his disciples said to him, "Lord, teach us to pray."

LUKE 11:1

Lord, of the many things the disciples could have asked You to teach them, they asked You how to pray. How does a person talk with God? Your response is beautiful in simplicity, and it remains a model for my prayers today. So as I kneel before God, my Father, I'll offer up my praise. I'll surrender to His will. I'll ask for needs met; I'll ask for spiritual debts forgiven. I'll commit to treating others as He treats me. I'll plead for a life free from the pull of sin. Lord, thank You for Your words that guide me through prayer. Amen.

THINK ABOUT IT:

Read Christ's prayer in Matthew 6 and Luke 11.
What does it teach you about praying?

Please God!

Do you think I am trying to make people accept me? No, God is the One I am trying to please. Am I trying to please people? If I still wanted to please people, I would not be a servant of Christ.

GALATIANS 1:10 NCV

God, Your will often goes against the grain of society. What You ask me to do may seem absurd to nonbelievers. Yet You are so much wiser than the world. You see clearly everything that is to come, and You have my best-case path in mind as You lead me. It is to You I owe my allegiance and look to for approval. But God, I still struggle with pleasing people. I want to fit in. In those moments when I feel myself bending toward the world, pull me back to You. Remind me of all I know to be true. You are Lord, and I will please You. Amen.

THINK ABOUT IT:

How do your everyday choices shift when
you become a God pleaser?

Ordered

For God is not a God of confusion but of peace....
All things should be done decently and in order.

1 CORINTHIANS 14:33, 40

God, Paul's orderly model for the church in Corinth can serve equally as a model for day-to-day living. Without Your character flowing through all the church did, there would have been little benefit to the Gospel. Your nature being mirrored in the Corinthians was vital then, and it remains vital for me now. I know all too well how confusion feels. It muddles my thinking and blurs my purpose. I'm not as fruitful in chaos, God. Still the turmoil, please. Let everything fall into its proper place. Help me order my days so that I can be at my best. . .so I can reflect You best. Amen.

THINK ABOUT IT:

Where can you bring more of God's harmony into your life?

Don't Forget

When you eat all you want and build nice houses and live in them, when your herds and flocks grow large and your silver and gold increase, when you have more of everything, then your heart will become proud. You will forget the LORD your God.

DEUTERONOMY 8:12–14 NCV

Father, may I take this warning to heart; may the truth of its words never become the pattern of my life. Because it is so true, so humbling, so frightening. The more that fills my life, the more likely I am to ignore You. Forgive me for those times! Nothing is more valuable than You. Everything comes from You. I thank You for the many blessings You have given me. Use them to point me to You and snuff out my pride in what *I* gain. Amen.

THINK ABOUT IT:

Why do possessions sometimes crowd out
God and make room for pride?

Seize the Day

So watch your step. Use your head. Make the most of every chance you get. These are desperate times! Don't live carelessly, unthinkingly. Make sure you understand what the Master wants.

EPHESIANS 5:15–17 MSG

Father, it is so easy to get wrapped up in the day-to-day, so easy to get caught up in emotion and decide to go one way or another, do one thing or another, without seeing You in the process. You offer me Your wisdom and direction. . .why do I not come to You more often? I only have a set number of days to live out Your will here on earth. Help me as Your Word says to make the most of them. I don't want to waste opportunities to be a witness to You. I don't want to stray from Your purposes. May I pause first and think on You before moving forward. Amen.

THINK ABOUT IT:

What distracts you from the goal of living every moment for God?

Mighty Small Faith

He said to them, "...For truly, I say to you, if you have faith like a grain of mustard seed, you will say to this mountain, 'Move from here to there,' and it will move, and nothing will be impossible for you."

MATTHEW 17:20

God, no matter what size my faith, You have the power to accomplish great things in and through me. When I am in Your will, nothing is impossible for me because nothing is impossible for You in achieving Your purposes. What appear to be mountains in my life are just molehills in Your sight. That sin I struggle with...a friend I'm afraid to witness to...the times this world calls my beliefs into question and I feel weak to remain rooted in You... With Your power I can command "mountains." Please never let me forget it! Amen.

THINK ABOUT IT:

What obstacles can you face with new confidence
when you internalize Christ's words in Matthew?

Mind Changer

*But Moses implored the LORD his God and said, "O LORD, why does
your wrath burn hot against your people, whom you have brought
out of the land of Egypt with great power and with a mighty
hand?"... And the LORD relented from the disaster
that he had spoken of bringing on his people.*

EXODUS 32:11, 14

God, what an amazing thought! You listen to believers. You hear what
I whisper in my heart or cry out loud. Like a good father, You won't
always do what I say, but You will receive my prayers. And sometimes,
as Moses experienced, You will change Your mind. Even in hopeless
situations, remind me to never stop *asking*...to never stop approaching
You with reverence and faith. You will always do what's best. Thank You
for being such an amazing God! Amen.

THINK ABOUT IT:

Does Moses' example give you a renewed
sense of the power of prayer?

Better Than

For a day in your courts is better than a thousand elsewhere. I would rather be a doorkeeper in the house of my God than dwell in the tents of wickedness. For the LORD God is a sun and shield; the LORD bestows favor and honor. No good thing does he withhold from those who walk uprightly. O LORD of hosts, blessed is the one who trusts in you!

PSALM 84:10-12

Father, this world is all I really know. I have the promise of heaven, but until then, my reality is the here and now. When I am tempted to make choices based solely on today, speak the truth of this psalm to my heart. One day with You is better than a thousand anywhere else. Your blessings are beyond anything this world could offer. May I never stop short of the promise. Amen.

THINK ABOUT IT:

Does shortsightedness impact how you live for God—that is, living in the moment versus living for eternity?

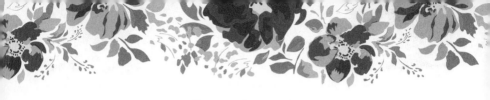

On a Mission

And when his parents saw him, they were astonished. And his mother said to him, "Son, why have you treated us so? Behold, your father and I have been searching for you in great distress." And he said to them, "Why were you looking for me? Did you not know that I must be in my Father's house?"

LUKE 2:48-49

Lord, I sometimes feel lost in where I should be and what I should be doing for You. I'm more like Mary—frantic, missing the big picture— when You knew precisely what Your purpose was and how You should go about it. I'll never have Your clear vision on my own, Lord. Please reveal Your plan in Your time. Nudge me toward the *where* and *what*. At the end of each day, and at the end of my life, I want to be found doing my Father's will. Amen.

THINK ABOUT IT:

Are you confident in your calling? If not, how can you carve out time to seek God's direction?

Above and Beyond

"And if anyone forces you to go one mile, go with him two miles.
Give to the one who begs from you, and do not refuse
the one who would borrow from you."

MATTHEW 5:41-42

Lord, You call me to be stingy in grudges and generous in love. You know I struggle with this at times. My default is to protect my own interests, especially when someone treats me badly. Help me model my character after You. You are the greatest example of responding sacrificially. You were condemned and abused, yet You held nothing back, even Your life, to benefit those who nailed You to the cross. Be with me as I go that extra mile, as I give with open hands, just as You did for me. Amen.

THINK ABOUT IT:

Why is it so difficult to turn the other cheek when wronged?
How does Christ's example and presence enable you to do just that?

Sequoia-Like

*As you received Christ Jesus the Lord, so continue to live in him.
Keep your roots deep in him and have your lives built on him.
Be strong in the faith, just as you were taught, and always be thankful.*

COLOSSIANS 2:6-7 NCV

Lord, when I first turned to You, my new life was like a sapling. With shallow roots, it would have been easy to pull out. But You have grown me through Your Word and through Your tender care. I'll continue to grow with You, Lord. Each day I want my spiritual roots to go deeper still. Redwoods aren't easily uprooted. . .and neither is a life planted firmly in You! It is able to withstand the harshest winds; it is a beautiful reflection of You. Thank You for all You do to keep me rooted. Amen.

THINK ABOUT IT:

What do you do to remain rooted in Christ?

A Good Name

Now there was in Joppa a disciple named Tabitha, which, translated, means Dorcas. She was full of good works and acts of charity.

ACTS 9:36

Father, I sometimes wonder what others will remember about how I lived. I hope that I am building a reputation like Tabitha. How beautiful that she was known for doing good—and not just a little bit; she was *full* of charity. The widows wept at her death, recalling all she had done. More beautiful than this is the fact that You used her life to lead others to faith. Father, fill me with a desire to reach out in kindness, to let my life tell of Your truth. May it be said of me that I was filled with good works—that through Your work in me, others believed. Amen.

THINK ABOUT IT:

What ways are you like—or can become like—Tabitha?

Such a Time

Then Mordecai told them to reply to Esther, "...if you keep silent at this time, relief and deliverance will rise for the Jews from another place, but you and your father's house will perish. And who knows whether you have not come to the kingdom for such a time as this?"

ESTHER 4:13-14

God, You have every last detail mapped out. No matter how confusing this world becomes, I can rest knowing Your plan will unfold—perfectly. And rather than working alone from heaven, You include Your children in what moves Your plan forward here on earth. Even in my weakness, You can use me! You have me right where I need to be to fit into Your plan—perfectly. When I am hesitant to act—when I'm on the verge of keeping silent like Esther—remind me of the honor and blessing of risking all for You. Amen.

THINK ABOUT IT:

How have you seen God's perfect timing in your life? In others'?

Wardrobe Staples

Stand therefore, having fastened on the belt of truth, and having put on the breastplate of righteousness, and, as shoes for your feet, having put on the readiness given by the gospel of peace. In all circumstances take up the shield of faith, with which you can extinguish all the flaming darts of the evil one; and take the helmet of salvation, and the sword of the Spirit, which is the word of God.

Ephesians 6:14-17

God, as I get dressed each morning, don't let me walk out the door before I put on my most important "accessories." More than adornment, Your armor is essential. Without it, I'm left bare to Satan's assault, the evil that tries to hinder my walk with You. But with it, I am ready to face the day—not just with style—but with Your truth, righteousness, peace, faith, salvation, and words. Amen.

THINK ABOUT IT:

How does God's armor equip you for daily
spiritual battles against Satan?

Look Ahead

The sun had risen on the earth when Lot came to Zoar. Then the
LORD rained on Sodom and Gomorrah sulfur and fire from
the LORD out of heaven. . . . But Lot's wife, behind him,
looked back, and she became a pillar of salt.

GENESIS 19:23-24, 26

God, when You call me to new life in You, You call me to leave behind my old life of sin—for my good! While on the surface sin is attractive, it is also deadly. Through obedience I will thrive. If Satan tempts me to look back longingly, keep my eyes riveted on You, God. Looking forward to eternity with You is worth much more than any backward glance. In "giving up" the past, I have only to gain. Amen.

THINK ABOUT IT:

How do prayer and spending time in God's
word help diminish the pull to disobey?

Elephantine Memory

The LORD answers, "Can a woman forget the baby she nurses?
Can she feel no kindness for the child to which she gave birth?
Even if she could forget her children, I will not forget
you. See, I have written your name on my hand."
ISAIAH 49:15-16 NCV

Lord, You have designed a loving bond between mother and child. After nine months of pregnancy and then years of tender care as the child grows, a mother isn't likely to forget. It *seems* unthinkable. Your promise to remember Your children goes even further. It *is* unthinkable; You will never forget, Lord. When I feel insignificant, just one of many billions lost in a crowd, You remember me still. I am precious to You, so much so that You died on the cross to bring me life. May I never forget Your love. Amen.

THINK ABOUT IT:

Do the words of Isaiah change how you see yourself?

Celebrate!

Then Miriam the prophetess, the sister of Aaron, took a tambourine in her hand, and all the women went out after her with tambourines and dancing. And Miriam sang to them: "Sing to the LORD, for he has triumphed gloriously; the horse and his rider he has thrown into the sea."

EXODUS 15:20-21

Lord, these verses lift my spirit. I can almost feel the celebration in the words. You brought victory, and Miriam and the other women were ready to rejoice. Out of tune or not, it's time for me to sing to You, Lord. Today and every day is a chance to offer praise for all You've done—and are yet to do. I'll lift my voice in song; I'll move with joy in dance. Because You are glorious, Lord. You are glorious! Amen.

THINK ABOUT IT:

When was the last time you let go and celebrated God through music or dancing?

By Example

Therefore, since we are surrounded by so great a cloud of witnesses,
let us also lay aside every weight, and sin which clings so closely,
and let us run with endurance the race that is set before us.

Father, thank You for so many people who show what it means to follow You each day. Thank You for giving me examples in Your Word of faith lived out. It's no secret that the faith path gets bumpy. When I wear down, I look to You; I look to Your presence in those who have gone before and shined! I'm in the race, Father. Show me what entangles me, trips me. I'm determined to run my best for You. And I know You cheer me on as I take each step in faith. Amen.

THINK ABOUT IT:

Who is in your own "cloud of witnesses"?
How do their lives motivate you?

Unto Him

Now unto him that is able to keep you from falling, and to present you faultless before the presence of his glory with exceeding joy, to the only wise God our Saviour, be glory and majesty, dominion and power, both now and ever. Amen.

JUDE 24–25 KJV

Lord God, I kneel today with Jude's words in my mind as a beautiful reflection of the prayer in my own soul, because more and more I realize that You are *all* to me. Without You I'd stumble, but You uphold me. Without You I'd have no hope of heaven, but You offer grace; You'll present me in eternity with Your righteousness as mine, and not with reluctance but with *exceeding joy*. Such an amazing thought! God, You alone are worthy—worthy of all glory, all majesty, all dominion, all power—for all time. Amen.

THINK ABOUT IT:

How can you honor God for all He means to you?

Scripture Index

Bible Encouragement for Your Heart

Read through the Bible in a Year Devotional

This lovely devotional features a simple plan for reading through the Bible in one year with an accompanying devotional thought inspired by that day's Bible reading. Each day's devotion will encourage you to read a passage from the Old Testament, New Testament, and Psalms or Proverbs and provides a relevant spiritual takeaway for practical, everyday living.

DiCarta / 978-1-68322-756-4 / $16.99

Pray through the Bible in a Year Devotional

This deluxe devotional features a plan for reading through the Bible in a year with an accompanying prayer inspired by that day's scripture reading—just for you.

DiCarta / 978-1-64352-330-9 / $16.99